Practical
KOREAN
COOKING

by Noh Chin-hwa
Copyreader: Shirley A. Dorow

HOLLYM

Elizabeth, NJ · Seoul

Practical Korean Cooking

Copyright © 1985
by Hollym Corporation; Publishers

First published in 1985
Twentieth printing, 2005
by Hollym International Corp.
18 Donald Place, Elizabeth, New Jersey 07208, U.S.A.
Phone: (908) 353-1655   Fax: (908) 353-0255
http://www.hollym.com

Published simultaneously in Korea
by Hollym Corporation; Publishers
13-13 Gwancheol-dong, Jongno-gu, Seoul 110-111, Korea
Phone: (02) 735-7551~4   Fax: (02) 730-5149, 8192
http://www.hollym.co.kr e-mail: info@hollym.co.kr

ISBN: 0-930878-37-x
Library of Congress Catalog Card Number: 85-80492

Printed in Korea

CONTENTS

INTRODUCTION

This cookbook of Korean recipes in English has been prepared for the English reader with the hope that westerner cooks might experience truly authentic Korean dishes. Until now many Korean cookbooks have been presented in English, but they present only those recipes which westerners are presumed to prefer and they modify the recipes for western taste.

This cookbook is authentically Korean. It is a careful translation of recipes prepared by a woman who directs a Korean cooking school in Seoul, Korea for real Korean housewives who are actually using these recipes daily. Even the Korean style layout of the book is the same style as in Korean cookbooks and magazine cooking columns today.

It is true that these recipes stem from age-old Korean traditional recipes and as such are scintillating combinations of food and seasoning unique to the Korean heritage. It is also true, however, that Korean cooking is known for its individual touches. Each family has its own way of seasoning, and brides new to a certain family live with the mother-in-law, even today, long enough to learn these subtle nuances in cooking for their husbands.

The western reader, too, may wish to vary the ingredients according to individual taste. This is acceptable Korean-style cooking. However the recipes presented here present the current vogue based on years of refinement by the collective Korean palate.

Some of these recipes are presented in English for the first time. The step-by-step photo sequences make preparation quite easy and the glossary will help readers understand each individual ingredient and thereby develop a feel for the total impact intended in each recipe.

This book is presented in the hope that gourmet cooks interested in Oriental cookery may extend their repertoire of truly good food and enjoy authentic Korean cooking.

Seoul, Korea

Shirley A. Darow

PREPARATION TIPS

Korean food preparation methods are quite different from western ones. The main jobs in preparing a Korean meal are the cutting, slicing, seasoning and careful arranging of the food.

The cutting of foods before cooking is very important for appearance as well as convenience in eating with chopsticks. Slicing, chopping, scoring and sectioning the vegetables, fish and meat are techniques employed so that the food will cook quickly and be easier to eat. Also, each ingredient is cut or sliced into the same size or shape and the same thickness so that it cooks evenly and looks neat. Because of the quick cooking the nutritional value remains high as well. Scoring, which is the process of cutting slits in the meat, allows the marinade to penetrate further into meats and also prevents the cooked meat from curling up during cooking. Chopping the seasonings (such as garlic, green onion and ginger) allows for better distribution of the flavor throughout the dish.

Various seasoning sauces are used for marinating meat or fish before broiling or stir-frying. Other sauces are used on vegetables. The amounts of seasonings used may vary with one's preference and other ingredients may also be added to suit one's individual taste.

Some of the sauces are these:

1. Seasoning soy sauce: Combine 4 tbsp. soy sauce, 2 tbsp. sugar, 1 tbsp. rice wine, 1 tbsp. chopped green onion, 1 tbsp. chopped garlic, 1 tbsp. sesame oil, 1 tbsp. sesame salt (crushed sesame that has been toasted with a little salt added), and black pepper to taste. Pine nuts and extra rice wine are optional.

2. Sweet sauce: Combine 1 cup soy sauce, ½ lb. dark corn syrup, ⅓ cup sugar, ⅔ cup water, 1 tbsp. ginger juice or flat slices of fresh ginger, ¼ cup rice wine, 1 tsp. black pepper, and a little MSG in a pan and simmer on low heat until thick.

3. Vinegar-soy sauce: Combine 4 tbsp. soy sauce, 1 tsp. sugar, ½ tbsp. sesame salt, 2 tsp. vinegar, chopped green onion and garlic to taste.

4. Mustard-vinegar sauce: Slowly stir ½ cup boiling water into 7 tbsp. mustard powder; stir until a smooth paste forms in the bowl. Put the bowl containing the mustard paste upside down on a hot cooking pot (perhaps one where rice is cooking) and let it stand for 10-15 minutes. When the mustard is somewhat translucent add 1 tbsp. soy sauce, 3 tbsp. sugar, ½ cup vinegar and 1 tsp. salt and mix well.

5. Seasoned red pepper paste: Combine 2 tbsp. red pepper paste, 2 tbsp. soy sauce, 1 tbsp. chopped garlic, 2 tbsp. chopped green onion, 1 tbsp. sugar, 1 tbsp. sesame salt, and 2 tbsp. sesame oil in a pan and simmer on low heat until thick.

The final step in preparing most dishes is the careful arranging of the foods paying particular attention to alternating the natural colors of the foods to make a pleasant pattern. Foods are always arranged neatly in concentric circles, radial designs or parallel linear columns and never placed in a disorderly fashion. The dish must have eye appeal when presented for eating and recipes often give directions for the exact arrangement of the foods. The photos illustrate this important part of Korean cookery clearly as well.

The recipes in this book will generally serve 4-6 persons.

In the recipes in this book quantities are given in American standard cup and spoon measurements and metric measure for weight.

THE KOREAN DIET

For centuries the Koreans have eaten the fruits of the sea, the field and the mountain because these are the geographically significant features of the Korean peninsula.

The Yellow Sea and Sea of Japan offer excellent fish, seaweed and shellfish for the Korean table. The lowland fields produce excellent grains and vegetables while the uplands grow marvelous fruits and nuts—apple, pear, plum, chestnut, walnut, pine nut and persimmon to name a few. And the ever-present mountains offer wild and cultivated mushrooms, roots and greens. A temperate climate makes for four seasons with the fall harvest being the most abundant.

Through the centuries the basic seasonings—red pepper, green onion, soy sauce, bean pastes, garlic, ginger, sesame, mustard, vinegar and wines—have been combined various ways to enhance the meats, fish, seafood and vegetables in the peculiarly spicy and delicious Korean manner. Various regions of Korea have special seasoning combinations—some hotter, some spicier—and each family also has its particular seasoning pattern. One family uses no salted shrimp juice in kimchi; another uses a great deal, but both claim kimchi as an integral part of their daily diet.

Kimchi is a kind of a spicy fermented pickle and accompanies every Korean meal. It is made from cabbage, turnip, cucumber or seasonable vegetables, seasoned with red pepper, garlic, onion, ginger, salt, oysters and soused salted fish juice, and fermented in an earthenware crock. Kimchi is made in large quantities in late autumn for use during the winter months. Autumn kimchi making is called kimjang which is one of Korea's most important household events. Kimchi contains good amounts of vitamin C and stimulates the appetite. Somehow, kimchi and rice make an excellent flavor and texture combination.

The basic diet includes at each meal steamed rice, hot soup, kimchis and a number of meat and/or vegetable side dishes with fruit as an after-meal refresher. In-season fresh vegetables are used at the peak of their season and dried or preserved for out-of-season use later on.

Korean table settings are classified into the 3-chop, the 5-chop, the 7-chop, the 9-chop and the 12-chop setting according to the number of side dishes served. The average family takes three or four side dishes along with rice, soup and kimchi for an everyday Korean meal.

When a family entertains guests for a special occasion, such as a wedding celebration or 60th birthday party, a dozen or more delightful dishes of different kinds are served according to the season. In addition, there is a characteristic way of setting the table for each occasion: New Year's Day Table, Moon-Festival Day Table, Baby's First Birthday Table, Ancestor-Memorial Day Table, Bride's Gift Table or Drinking Table.

Korean food is usually shared by diners. Each person has his own bowl of rice and soup, but other dishes are set on the table for all to reach. The main dishes and the side dishes are distinguished by the quantities served. At meal time, the smaller quantity of the food served will be one of the side dishes. Larger quantity dishes will be the main dish and nothing more will be needed except rice and kimchi.

As for the serving, all the food dishes except hot soups are set at one time on a low table that is set on the floor; at which one sits to eat. The main dishes and the side dishes which are shared by all are placed in the middle of the table. The rice and soup are placed in front of each diner. Chopsticks and spoons are used for eating.

In general the Korean diet is high in grains and vegetables which add much fiber to the diet, moderate but adequate in protein, both animal and vegetable (bean curd, bean sprouts, bean pastes, soy bean sauce), moderate in calories and low in fat and sugar. In short—a very healthy, well-balanced diet. It may be a bit high in salt if soy sauce is used heavily. It may or may not be red peppery hot; it is a matter of individual taste.

The Korean diet is changing and developing but basically the diet pattern has remained the same. Westerners may do well to examine this diet pattern and shift to a similar diet pattern for their own long and healthy life.

Meats
Poultry

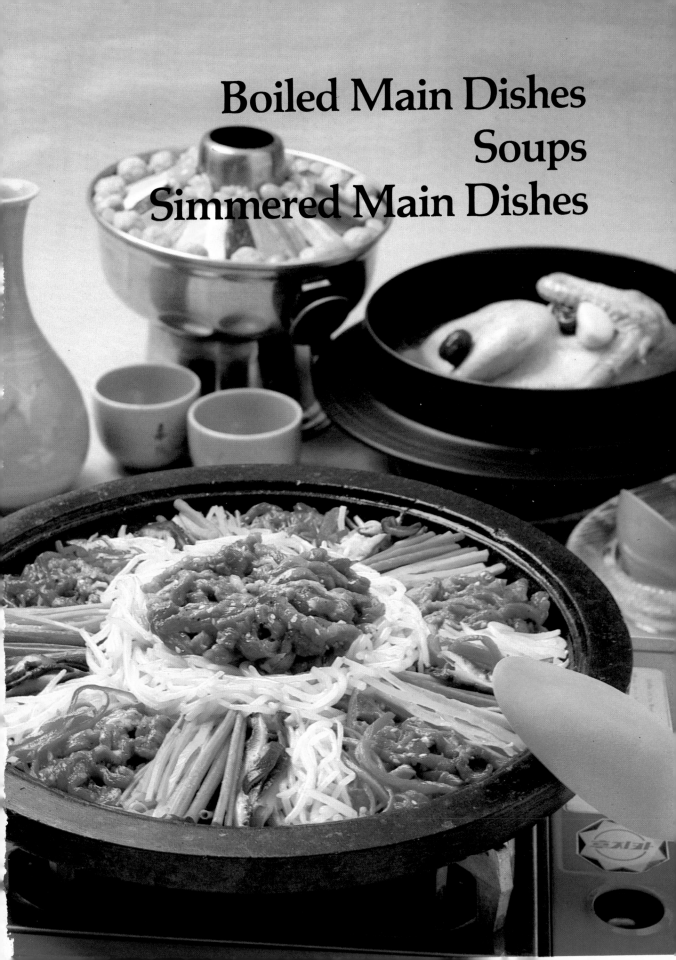

Boiled Main Dishes
Soups
Simmered Main Dishes

Beef Stock Soup
Komt'ang (곰탕)

Ingredients 1⅓ lb. shank of beef, ½ whole Korean white radish, ¼ lb. Chinese noodles, 1 large green onion, 5 cloves garlic, salt, black pepper, MSG
Method 1 Cut the beef into large pieces and halve the radish. Boil the beef and radish in 30 cups of water. Lower the heat and simmer for 1 hour until the meat is very tender.

2 Take the meat and radish out of the broth. Cool the broth and skim off excess fat that has floated to the top. Slice the meat thinly into bite-sized pieces cutting against the grain. Slice the radish into pieces ⅛" thick.

3 Add the meat, radish and crushed garlic to the broth. Then bring to a boil again.

4 Cut large green onion into rings. Add the salt, black pepper and green onion and check the seasoning just before serving.

Hint This beef stock soup may be made using the knuckle bone.

Cut the meat into large pieces.

2 Halve the whole radish.

3 Remove the meat and radish from the broth when cooked.

4 Strain the broth to remove excess fat.

5 Slice thinly cutting against the grain.

6 Boil the meat and radish in the broth.

Beef Rib Soup
Kalbit'ang (갈비탕)

Ingredients   1⅓ lb. beef, ⅓ Korean white radish, green onion, garlic, 1 egg, 1 tbsp. soy sauce, salt, black pepper, MSG, 15 cups broth

Method   **1** Cut the ribs into pieces 1⅔″ long and score them at ⅓″ intervals. Halve the white radish lengthwise.

2 Fry the beaten, salted yolk and white of egg separately into sheets and cut into thin strips. Chop the green onion and garlic finely.

3 Boil the ribs and radish with 30 cups of water in a large pot. Remove the radish from the broth when cooked and simmer the ribs for about 2 hours until very tender.

4 Take the ribs out of the broth and slice the radish thinly. Then mix the ribs and radish with the soy sauce, black pepper, sesame oil, green onion and garlic.

5 Cool the broth and skim off excess fat from the top.

6 Put the seasoned ribs and radish into the broth and bring to a boil again. Season with black pepper and MSG.

7 Check the seasoning and place the beef rib soup in each bowl. Garnish with egg strips.

Hint   **1** Scoring the ribs cross-grain makes them easier to eat.

2 The soup may be saltier when cooled, so add salt sparingly when seasoning.

1 Score the ribs.

2 Fry the beaten yolk and white of egg separately into thin sheets.

3 Season the ribs and radish.

4 Boil the seasoned ribs and radish in the broth.

Beef Rib Soup

Spicy Beef Soup
Yukkaejang (육개장)

Ingredients   ½ lb. beef, ½ lb. tripe, ½ lb. small beef intestine, ⅓ lb. fern bracken, 4 large green onions, black pepper, MSG, seasoning sauce: (3 tbsp. red pepper paste, 9 cloves garlic, 5 tbsp. sesame salt, sesame oil, 4 tbsp. red pepper powder, 4 tbsp. salad oil), 15 cups broth

Method   **1** Wash the beef.
2 Wash and soak the tripe in hot water. Then scrape off the black skin with the back of a knife.
3 Remove any fat from the small intestine and cut it into pieces. Wash the pieces clean scrubbing with coarse salt.
4 Simmer the beef, tripe and small intestine in 30 cups of water for 2 hours until very tender.

5 Shred the beef into thick strips. Cut the tripe into pieces 2¾″ long and ¼″ wide. Cut the small intestine into bite-sized pieces.
6 Clean the bracken and green onions and cut them into 4¾″ lengths.
7 Put the above ingredients (except the green onions) in a bowl and mix them with the seasoning sauce.
8 Mix and fry the oil and red pepper powder in a pan to make the red pepper oil.
9 Add the **#7** seasoned ingredients and 15 cups of the broth to the pan and bring to a boil. Add the green onion slices and boil slightly again.

1 Remove any fat from the beef intestine.

2 Mix the bracken, onion, meat and small intestine with the seasoning.

3 Make the red pepper oil.

4 Add the broth and **#2** to **#3** and bring to a boil.

Spicy Beef Soup

15

Meatball Soup
Wanjakuk (완자국)

1 Finely mince the beef.

2 Wrap the bean curd in a cloth and squeeze it tightly.

3 Sieve the mashed bean curd.

4 Mix the meat and bean curd with the seasoning.

5 Shape the mixture into meatballs 1″ in diameter.

6 Add the meatballs dipped into beaten egg to the boiling broth.

Ingredients ¼ lb. ground beef, garland chrysanthemum, ½ square onion, 1 egg, ½ tsp. salt, ½ tsp. soy sauce, ½ tsp. sesame oil, ½ tsp. sesame salt, 2 tbsp. flour, 7 cups broth

Method 1 Chop the beef and garlic finely.
2 Wrap the bean curd in a clean cloth and squeeze out the excess water. Sieve the mashed bean curd.
3 Mix #1 and #2 with the soy sauce, salt and sesame salt.
4 Shape the #3 mixture into meatballs 1″ in diameter. Dip each meatball into flour.
5 Pour the broth into a pan and season it with soy sauce and salt.

When the broth boils, add the meatballs dipped into beaten egg and bring to a boil again. Float the garland chrysanthemum leaves on the top and serve.

Hint 1 Use finely ground or minced beef so that the meatballs will not break.
2 Oil both hands to form well-rounded meatballs.

16

Spring Chicken Soup
Yŏnggyebaeksuk (영계백숙)

Ingredients   1 spring chicken, ½ cup glutinous rice, 10 cloves garlic, 6 jujubes, 6 chestnuts, 1 knob ginger, salt, black pepper, MSG

Method   **1** Remove the organs, lower legs, feet and head from the chicken and clean.
2 Stuff the chicken cavity with the glutinous rice and 5 cloves of garlic. Sew the body cavity shut.
3 Put the stuffed chicken in a pot and add water enough to simmer. Add the jujubes, peeled chestnuts, ginger and remaining cloves of garlic. Cover the pot and bring to a boil. Then reduce the heat and simmer for 1 hour.
4 Add the salt, black pepper and sliced green onion just before eating.

Hint   **1** Stuff the chicken cavity with only a little glutinous rice, leaving room for it to expand as it cooks.
2 For medicinal use, take the boiled chicken out of the broth, add ginseng root and simmer the broth again.

1 Stuff the chicken cavity with the glutinous rice and garlic.

2 Sew the body cavity shut.

3 Add water enough to simmer.

Fancy Hot Pot
Shinsöllo (신선로)

Ingredients   **A** ⅓ lb. ground beef, 3 tbsp. cornstarch powder, 1 egg, various seasonings
B   ¼ lb. beef liver, ¼ lb. white fish fillets, ½ tsp. salt, ½ tsp. black pepper, flour, 1 egg
C   2 eggs, 2 oz. carrot, 3 dried brown, oak mushrooms, ½ bundle watercress, flour, 30 gingko nuts, 5 walnuts, 5 stone mushrooms
D   2 oz. beef strips, ½ round onion, 1 dried brown, oak mushroom

Method   **1** Mix the ground beef, cornstarch powder and egg with various seasonings reserving one-third of the mixture for meatballs.

2 Heat a well-oiled square fry pan. Spread the **#1** mixture on the hot pan and fry it until well-done. Then cut the fried meat mixture into bite-sized pieces. Use the reserved one-third of the meat mixture to form meatballs ⅓″ in diameter. Dip each ball in flour and beaten egg and brown in oil.

3 Slice the liver flatly and soak it in cold water to remove the blood. Season the liver slices with the **B** ingredients and dip them into flour, then into beaten egg and brown in oil.

4 Slice the fish into bite-sized pieces and mix it with the **B** seasonings. Dip each piece into flour and then

5 Add the fried liver slices.

6 Garnish the top with the gingko nuts, walnuts and meatballs.

18

into beaten egg and brown in oil.

5 Slice 2 oz. beef, ½ round onion and 1 dried mushroom into thin strips and mix them with the seasonings. Layer them in the bottom of the shinsollo pot.

6 Make a second layer with the fried liver, fish and meat slices.

7 Cut the carrot into the same lengths as the radius of the shinsollo pot and ½″ wide.

8 After soaking the dried mushrooms in water, squeeze out the excess water. Cut them into the same size as the carrot rectangles.

9 Remove the leaves from the watercress and skewer the stems together evenly.

10 Soak the shelled walnuts in hot water, drain and peel off the dark skin.

11 Fry the shelled ginko nuts slightly in a greased pan and remove the skins chafing them with a clean paper.

12 Dip the #9 skewered watercress into flour and then into beaten egg and brown in oil.

13 Fry the beaten egg yolk and white separately into thin sheets. Cut the egg sheets into the same size as the carrot rectangles.

14 Arrange the prepared vegetable and egg rectangles attractively alternating colors in a spoke fashion on top of the other layers. Garnish with the gingko nuts, walnuts and meatballs.

15 Add meat broth to the shinsollo and heat, or add water to the shinsollo and bring it to a quick boil; serve and eat. (The shinsollo pan may be heated with charcoal or canned heat in its center core.)

1 Mix the ground beef, cornstarch powder and egg with the seasonings.

2 Fry the meat mixture in a square fry pan.

3 Cut the fried meat mixture into bite-sized pieces.

4 Place a layer of the seasoned beef, onion and mushrooms in the bottom.

Method for Vegetable-Beef Simmered Dish

1 Mix the sliced beef with the seasonings.

2 Remove the seeds from the peppers and slice them into thin strips.

3 Mix the sliced onion, dried mushrooms and beef with the seasonings.

4 Arrange all the sliced ingredients alternating colors.

5 Place the mung-bean sprouts and beef in the center.

6 Pour the hot meat-broth over the top.

Ingredients   1 lb. beef, 7 dried brown, oak mushrooms, ¼ carrot, ⅓ lb. mung-bean sprouts, 2 oz. small green onion, 3 red peppers, 1 round onion, 1 tbsp. sugar, 1 tbsp. rice wine, 3 tbsp. soy sauce, 1 tbsp. sesame salt, 2 tbsp. chopped green onion, 2 tsp. garlic, black pepper, salt, MSG

Method   1 Cut the beef into thin strips, mix with the seasonings and let it stand. Slice the round onion into thin strips.

2 Soak the dried mushrooms in

Vegetable-Beef Simmered Dish
Soegogi Chŏn-gol (쇠고기 전골)

water and remove the stems. Slice thinly and fry them lightly with the sesame oil, soy sauce and sugar.

3 Remove the beans and hair-like tips from the mung-bean sprouts and scald them slightly. Drain and mix them with the salt and sesame oil.

4 Cut the carrots into thin strips 2″ long. Cut the small green onion into the same lengths.

5 Halve the red peppers, remove the seeds and cut the peppers into thin strips.

6 Place the sliced round onion, $1/6$ dried mushroom and $1/6$ beef in the center of the pot.

7 Pile the beef and bean sprouts in the center of the pan and colorfully arrange the carrot, small green onion, mung-bean sprouts, dried mushrooms, red peppers and beef around them.

8 Make meat broth and season it with the salt, black pepper and MSG. Add the meat broth to **#7** and boil briefly at the table.

Hint By marinating the beef in the sugar and rice wine first, the meat will be tender and will not give off an odor. Mung-bean sprouts do not remain tasty if rinsed in cold water.

Method for Beef Intestine Simmered Dish

1 Rub the intestine with salt to clean.

2 Soak the tripe in hot water to remove the black skin.

3 Remove the thick cabbage stems.

4 Season the tripe and intestine.

20

Beef Intestine Simmered Dish
Kopch'ang Chŏn-gol (곱창 전골)

Ingredients **A** 1 lb. beef small intestine, ½ lb. tripe, ½ lb. shank of beef, 2 large green onions
B 5 dried brown, oak mushrooms, ⅓ carrot, ¼ lb. cabbage, 2 round onions, ¼ lb. thick noodles, 4 cups broth, ½ oz. garland chrysanthemum
C 3 tbsp. red pepper paste, 2 tbsp. soy sauce, 2 tsp. sugar, 6 tbsp. green onion, 3 cloves garlic, 2 tbsp. sesame salt, 2 tsp. sesame oil, 2 tbsp. red pepper powder; final seasonings: (2 tbsp. soy sauce, 1 tsp. green onion, 1 clove garlic, 4 tbsp. anchovy broth, 2 tsp. sesame salt, black pepper)

Method **1** Remove any fat from the small intestine and wash it clean rubbing it with salt.
2 Soak the tripe in hot water and drain. Remove the black skin by scraping with a spoon and wash it clean.
3 Wash the shank of beef and cut it into bite-sized pieces.
4 Put the **#1**, **#2**, **#3** ingredients with 30 cups of water in a large pot. Bring to a boil on high heat and then simmer for 1 hour on medium heat until tender.
5 Take the meat out of the **#4** liquid and cut it into bite-sized pieces. Mix well with the **C** ingre-

dients and place it in a heavy, flat chongol pot.
6 Soak the dried mushrooms in water and remove the stems. Cut X slits on them.
7 Halve the carrot and cut it diagonally into crescent-shaped pieces.
8 Remove the stems from the cabbage and cut the leaves into ¾" × 1¼" pieces.
9 Cut the round onions into the same size as the carrot pieces.
10 Cook the thick noodles in boiling water and rinse them in cold water. Drain.
11 Arrange the **#6**, **#7**, **#8**, **#9** vegetables in the **#5** pot attractively. Pour 4 cups of the **#4** broth over the vegetables and bring to a boil. When the vegetables are tender, place the noodles in the center and sprinkle them with the final seasonings. Add garland chrysanthemum leaves on the top.

5 Cut the onion.

6 Arrange the ingredients in a shallow cooking pan.

Simmered Chicken Dish
Takkogi Chŏn-gol (닭고기 전골)

1 Remove the meat from the bones.

2 Fry the shelled ginko nuts with salt.

3 Place the hot ginko nuts on paper and rub off the skins.

4 Shape the sliced jellied potato-cake like maejagwa.

5 Season the chicken and dried mushrooms separately.

6 Place the chicken in the center of a shallow cooking pan.

Ingredients   ⅔ lb. chicken, 5 dried brown, oak mushrooms, ⅓ carrot, 2 oz. small green onions, 1 round onion, 2 oz. watercress, 2 oz. garland chrysanthemum, ⅓ lb. konyak: jellied potato-cake (used like a noodle), 20 gingko nuts, 2 eggs, 1 green onion, 4 cloves garlic, ginger juice, 2 tbsp. soy sauce, 1 tbsp. sesame oil, 1 tbsp. sesame salt, 1 tbsp. red pepper powder, 1½ tbsp. sugar, 1 tbsp. red pepper paste, salt, black pepper, MSG

Method   1 Prepare the legs and breast of the chicken by removing the meat from the bones and cutting it into thin strips. Simmer the bones to make the chicken broth.

2 Soak the dried mushrooms in water, remove the stems and cut them into thin strips. Cut the round onion and carrot into thin strips.

3 Cut the small green onions and watercress into 2″ lengths.

4 Peel and fry the gingko nuts in an oiled pan. Place them on paper and rub off the top-skins.

5 Cut the konyak into ⅛″ thick and ¾″×2¾″ pieces. Slit each piece down the center leaving the ends intact and twist one end through the slit to shape it like maejagwa, thin Korean cookies.

6 Mix the green onion, chopped garlic, soy sauce, black pepper, sesame oil and salt to make the seasoning sauce. Season the chicken and dried mushroom strips separately.

7 Place the seasoned chicken in the center of a shallow cooking pan, surrounded by the prepared vegetables. Pour the broth over the ingredients and bring to a boil. When the flavor has developed, add the ginko nuts and garland chrysanthemum and bring to a boil and serve.

Hint   The konyak is absorbed in this chicken dish making it more flavorful.

Stews
Stir-Fried Dishes
Soy-Sauce Glazed Dishes

Beef Rib Stew
Soegalbitchim (쇠갈비찜)

Ingredients   4 lb. beef ribs, 4½ tbsp. sugar, 3 tbsp. rice wine, ½ cup chopped green onion, 1 tbsp. garlic, 9 tbsp. soy sauce, 2 tbsp. sesame salt, 2 tbsp. sesame oil, black pepper, MSG, 2 carrots, 15 chestnuts, 20 gingko nuts, 10 jujubes, 1 Korean white radish, 2 round onions, 3 cups water, 3 tbsp. pine nuts

Method   **1** Have the butcher cut the ribs into pieces 2⅓" long. Wash and score them diagonally at ⅓" intervals. Marinate them in the sugar and rice wine for 10 minutes.

2 Mix the garlic, green onions, soy sauce, sesame salt, sesame oil, black pepper and MSG to make the seasoning sauce.

3 Cut the carrots and white radish into chestnut-sized pieces.

4 Peel the chestnuts and clean the jujubes.

5 Peel and fry the shelled ginko nuts in an oiled pan until they turn green. Rub off the top-skins.

6 Fry the **#3, #4** and **#5** ingredients lightly in an oiled pan.

7 Cut the remaining carrot and round onions into thin strips.

8 Place the **#7** ingredients in the bottom of a pan and make a second layer with the ribs dipped into the seasoning sauce, leaving the center empty. Add 3 cups of water and cover. Boil hard for 20 minutes and then simmer for 30 minutes on medium heat. Add the prepared gingko nuts and simmer for 10 minutes more.

9 When the ribs and other ingredients become tender, remove the lid and simmer them on high heat until glazed.

10. Arrange the **#9** food attractively on a plate and sprinkle with the finely chopped pine nuts.

Hint   **1** Though you cook a large quantity of ribs, 3 cups of water should be sufficient.

2 When the gingko nuts are cooked, add the broth and simmer on high heat.

1 Score the ribs diagonally at ⅓" intervals.

2 Marinate the ribs in the sugar and rice wine.

3 Cut the radish and carrots into chestnut-sized pieces.

24

4 Place the ribs dipped into the seasoning sauce on top of the onion.

5 Top the ribs with the garnish.

6 Simmer the ingredients on high heat until glazed.

Beef and Vegetable Stew
Soegogi Yach'aetchim (쇠고기 야채찜)

Ingredients **A** 1 lb. beef, 5 large cabbage leaves
B ½ cup cornstarch powder, ½ egg, 6 tbsp. chopped green onion, 2 tbsp. garlic, 1 tbsp. rice wine, 2 tbsp. soy sauce, ½ tbsp. sesame oil, 1 tbsp. sugar, 1 tbsp. sesame salt, 1 tsp. salt, black pepper, MSG
C ½ carrot, 2 green peppers, 2 oz. mung-bean sprouts, parsley, cherries
Method **1** Remove the vein stems from the cabbage leaves and cut the leaves into 4″ square pieces. Scald in salted boiling water and rinse them in cold water.
2 Cut the carrot into ¼″ thick pieces and scald and cut them into ¼″ cubes. Halve the green peppers to remove the seeds and cut them into ¼″ square pieces. Scald the mung-bean sprouts, squeeze and chop them finely.

3 Mix the minced beef and sliced vegetables well with the **B** ingredients. Shape the mixture into oval meatballs in the palm of your hand and dip them in starch powder.
4 Dip the insides of the cabbage leaves in cornstarch powder. Place each meatball in the cabbage leaf and wrap it into a small bundle.
5 Place the cabbage bundles in a steamer and steam for 15 minutes.

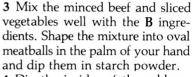

1 Remove the vein stems from the cabbage leaves.

2 Scald and cut the vegetables finely.

3 Stuff the meatballs into the leaves making small bundles.

4 Steam the cabbage bundles for 15 minutes.

Pork Rib Stew
Twaejigalbitchim (돼지갈비찜)

Ingredients **A** 1⅓ lb. pork ribs, 2 tbsp. salad oil
B 2½ tbsp. soy sauce, 1½ tbsp. sugar, 6 tbsp. green onion, 2 tbsp. garlic, 2 tbsp. ginger juice, 2 tbsp. rice wine
C pine nuts, ⅓ carrot, 20 gingko nuts, 2 potatoes, 2 green peppers, 2 jujubes

Method **1** Have the butcher cut the spareribs into 2″ long pieces and score them on both sides.
2 Stir-fry the ginko nuts in a lightly salted pan until they turn green color. Then rub off the top-skins.
3 Fry the spareribs in a heated oiled pan until brown.

Remove excess oil and place the ribs in another pan.
4 Add half of the mixed **B** ingredients and 2 cups water to the **#3** ribs and simmer them on high heat for 10 minutes.
5 When the ribs are tender, add the gingko nuts, the carrots and potatoes cut into flower shapes and the remaining seasoning and stir-fry until glazed.
6 Place the seasoned ribs and vegetables in a serving dish and garnish with the sliced jujube and powdered pine nuts.

2 Fry the ribs in a heated oiled pan until brown.

4 Add half of the **B** seasonings to **#3** and simmer.

1 Score the spareribs at ⅓″ intervals.

3 Place the ribs in another pan.

5 Add the remaining seasoning and stir, frying lightly.

Steamed Pork with Vegetables
Twaejigogi Saektchim (돼지고기 색찜)

Ingredients ⅔ lb. pork, ⅓ cucumber, ¼ carrot, 1 dried brown, oak mushroom, 2 stone mushrooms, egg sheets, salt, black pepper, 3 tbsp. sated shrimp juice, 1 tsp. ginger juice, MSG, pine nuts **Method** 1 Cut the pork (leaving on the fat) into pieces 3″×2″. Bind it tightly with a cotton thread and boil. Remove the fat from the boiled pork and trim it into a piece ⅛″ thick. Cut slits in the pork

and place on top of the piece of fat.
2 Cut the cucumber and carrot into thin strips and fry lightly. Fry the yolk and white of egg separately into sheets and cut them into thin strips.
3 Cut the dried mushroom and stone mushrooms into thin strips.
4 Place the above ingredients in the slits of the **#1** boiled pork alternating colors. Sprinkle the top evenly with salted shrimp juice and ginger juice and steam for 5 minutes.

1 Tie the pork with the cotton thread.

2 Cut slits in the boiled pork.

3 Cut the carrot into thin strips and fry.

4 Stuff the slits with the vegetables alternating colors.

5 Sprinkle the top with salted shrimp juice and ginger juice and steam.

Noodles with Beef and Vegetables
Soegogi Chapch'ae (쇠고기 잡채)

Ingredients **A** ⅓ lb. beef, 2 tbsp. soy sauce, 1 tbsp. sugar, 1 tbsp. green onion, 1 clove garlic, black pepper, 1 tbsp. sesame oil
B ⅓ lb. Chinese noodles (tangmyon), 1½ tbsp. soy sauce, 1 tbsp. sugar, 1 tbsp. sesame salt
C ⅓ carrot, 2 oz. bellflower roots, 1 clove garlic, ½ tsp. salt, 1 round onion, 5 dried brown, oak mushrooms, soy sauce, sugar, sesame oil, ½ bun-

dle watercress, 1 tsp. salt
D 1 egg, 1 stone mushroom, pine nuts
Method **1** Using tender beef, cut it into thin strips and let it stand in the **A** seasoning sauce.
2 Cut the carrot into thin strips and fry it lightly adding salt in an oiled pan.
3 Scald the bellflower roots in boiling water and shred them finely. Fry them lightly adding chopped

4 Scald the bellflower roots in boiling water.

1 Cut the beef into thin strips and marinate in the seasoning.

5 Scald Chinese noodles, drain and mix with sesame oil.

2 Cut the carrot into 2″ lengths.

6 Stir-fry the beef and then the dried mushrooms.

3 Stir-fry the carrot with salt.

7 Stir-fry all the ingredients lightly and season to taste.

garlic and salt.

4 Halve and cut the round onion into thin strips and fry adding salt.

5 Cut the watercress into 2″ lengths and fry lightly adding salt.

6 Cook Chinese noodles in boiling water until soft and rinse in cold water. Cut them into 8″ lengths and mix with sesame oil.

7 Fry the marinated beef with the dried mushrooms and sprinkle with sugar and soy sauce.

8 Stir-fry the **#6** noodles seasoning to taste with soy sauce, sugar and sesame salt. Combine all the pre-pared ingredients thoroughly and season with the sesame oil, black pepper and MSG.

9 Place the **#8** mixture on a plate and garnish with the egg yolk strips, stone mushroom strips and pine nuts.

Hint **1** When stir-frying each ingredient, begin with the light-colored ones. Fry the beef and dried mushroom last.

2 Add the watercress later so as to keep the fresh green color.

Stir-Fry Beef with Peppers
Soegogi P'utkoch'ubokkŭm (쇠고기 풋고추볶음)

Ingredients   ½ lb. beef tenderloin, 1 tbsp. rice wine, 2 tsp. soy sauce, ½ tsp. salt, 1 tsp. sugar, 1 tbsp. cornstarch powder, 3 oz. Korean green pepper, 3 red peppers, 3 cloves garlic, 1 tbsp. oil, 1 tsp. salt, ½ tsp. sugar

Method   1 Cut the beef into thin strips and season it with the rice wine, sugar, soy sauce, salt, and cornstarch powder. Let it stand for 10 minutes.
2 Cut the green peppers into thin strips and soak them in water to remove the "hot" taste.
3 Slice the garlic into flat pieces.
4 Stir-fry the green pepper and red pepper strips lightly with the salt and sugar in an oiled pan.
5 Stir-fry the garlic and seasoned beef in a lightly oiled pan. Add the #4 peppers and stir-fry again.

Hint   Fry the green peppers only slightly to keep the color clear. Green peppers contain much vitamin A.

1 Wash the sliced peppers and drain.

2 Fry the pepper lightly with the salt and sugar.

3 Fry the garlic, beef and add the #2 pepper mixture last of all.

Stir-Fry Rice Cake
Ttŏkpokkŭm (떡볶음)

Ingredients **A** ⅔ lb. rice cake
B ¼ lb. beef, 1 tbsp. soy sauce, ½ tbsp. sugar, 1 tbsp. green onion, 1 clove garlic, 1 tsp. sesame salt, ½ tbsp. sesame oil
C ¼ lb. carrot, 2 oz. bamboo shoots, 3 dried mushrooms, ½ cucumber, ½ cup water
D 1 tsp. soy sauce, ½ tbsp. sugar
Method **1** Cut the sticks of rice cake into 1⅔" lengths and divide them into lengthwise quar-

ters. Scald in boiling water and rinse in cold water.
2 Cut the beef into thick strips and season it with the **B** ingredients. Cut the carrots, bamboo shoots, dried mushrooms and cucumber into 1⅔" long, flat rectangles.
3 Fry the seasoned beef in a pan until cooked and add the vegetables, rice cake and water and bring to a boil. Season with the **D**

sugar and soy sauce and stir well.

1 Cut the sticks of rice cake into 1⅔" lengths and scald and rinse them in cold water.

2 Fry the green onion, garlic and beef and add the water.

3 Add the rice cake and vegetables to **#2** and cook briefly. Add the cucumber later and fry again lightly.

Stir-Fry Pork
Twaejigogibokkŭm (돼지고기볶음)

Ingredients ⅔ lb. pork, 1 round onion, 2 Korean green peppers, 2 Korean red peppers, 3 tbsp. oil, ¼ cup water, seasoning sauce: (2 tbsp. soy sauce, 1 tbsp. green onion, 1 tsp. garlic, 2 tbsp. red pepper paste, 1 knob ginger)

Method **1** Chop the ginger finely.
2 Cut the pork into 1⅔″ thick, flat pieces and mix it with the seasoning sauce.

3 Halve the green peppers, remove the seeds and cut them into piece ⅓″ × ½″. Cut the round onion into the same-sized pieces.
4 Fry the marinated pork in a heated oiled pan, add the above vegetables and stir-fry lightly.

Stir-Fry Pork with Vegetables

Stir-Fry Pork

Stir-Fry Pork with Vegetables
Twaejigogi Yach'aebokkŭm (돼지고기 야채볶음)

Ingredients ⅓ lb. pork, 3 tbsp. cornstarch powder, ¼ lb. carrot, 1 can of bamboo shoots, 3 dried brown, oak mushrooms, 1 round onion, ½ cucumber, 10 quail eggs, 2 tbsp. soy sauce, 1 tsp. green onion, 1 clove garlic, 1 tsp. ginger juice, salt, ½ tsp. sesame oil, 1 cup broth, 2 tbsp. cornstarch liquid

Method **1** Slice the pork thinly into pieces 2″ × ¾″. Sprinkle it with salt, black pepper and 3 tbsp. cornstarch powder.

2 Halve the carrot lengthwise and cut it diagonally into piece ¹/₁₀″ thick.

3 Cut the bamboo shoots and cucumber diagonally into crescent shapes.

4 Soften the dried mushrooms in water and remove the stems. Slice them into pieces ⅓″ wide.

5 Cut the round onion into thick strips.

6 Heat the oil in a pan. Then stir-fry the carrot, dried mushrooms, bamboo shoots, round onion and boiled quail eggs lightly adding them in order. Place them on a plate.

7 Re-oil the pan and stir-fry the garlic until savory. Then add the #1 pork and fry lightly.

8 Mix the #7 pork and the #6 ingredients. Season it with salt, soy sauce, sugar and ginger juice and fry again.

9 Pour the seasoned broth on this mixture and bring to a boil. Thicken the broth by pouring in 2 tbsp. starch liquid. Add the cucumber and sesame oil last of all.

Hint **1** Add the cucumber later to keep the color green. It changes to a yellow color if added first.

2 Add the sesame oil last to retain its special flavor and smell.

Method for Stir-Fry Pork with Vegetables

1 Sprinkle the bite-sized pieces of pork with the salt, black pepper and starch powder.

2 Stir-fry the carrot, dried mushroom, bamboo shoot, round onion and quail eggs in order.

3 Stir-fry the seasoned meat.

4 Mix **#2, #3** well and season with salt and soy sauce.

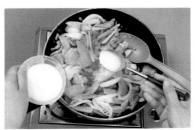

5 Add the starch liquid and broth to #4.

Method for Stir-Fry Pork

1 Cut the pork into 1⅔″ thick pieces and mix it with the seasoning sauce.

2 Cut the peppers and round onion into square pieces.

3 Stir-fry the marinated pork adding ½ cup water.

4 When almost cooked, add the **#2** vegetables and fry lightly.

Stir-Fry Pork with Kimchi

Twaejigogi Kimch'ibokkŭm (돼지고기 김치볶음)

Ingredients **A** ⅔ lb. pork (with fat and skin remaining), ⅔ lb. kimchi, 2 Korean green peppers, 1 red pepper, ½ round onion

B 3 tbsp. red pepper paste, 1 tbsp. chopped green onion, 1 tsp. sugar, sesame salt, black pepper, sesame oil, ½ tbsp. chopped garlic

Method 1 Cut the pork into flat pieces.

2 Combine the **B** ingredients to make the seasoned red pepper paste.

3 Add the #2 seasoned paste to the pork, mix well and allow it to stand for a while.

4 Remove the stuffing from the kimchi squeezing out the water. Slice it into flat pieces.

5 Halve the green peppers to remove the seeds and cut them into thick strips.

6 Cut the round onion into thin strips.

7 Fry the pork lightly first and then add the #4, #5, #6 ingredients and stir-fry once again.

Hint This food is delicious served with hot bean curd cut into small pieces.

1 Cut the pork into flat pieces.

3 Cut the green peppers into thin strips and the kimchi into flat pieces.

2 Combine the **B** ingredients to make the seasoned red pepper paste.

4 Fry the seasoned pork and then the sliced vegetables.

Broiled Chicken Giblets
Tangnaejangbokkŭm (닭내장볶음)

Ingredients   ⅔ lb. chicken gizzards and livers, 3 dried brown, oak mushrooms, ¼ lb. bamboo shoots, ⅓ lb. konyak: jellied potato-cake, 2 green bell peppers, 4 cloves garlic, 2 tbsp. salad oil, 2 tbsp. soy sauce, salt, ginger juice, black pepper, MSG, 2 tsp. cornstarch powder, ⅓ cup meat broth, 1 tbsp. rice wine, 1 tomato

Method   **1** Peel off the inner skin from the chicken gizzards and clean them by scrubbing with salt. Slit the outer part of the gizzards. Then cut them with the chicken livers into bite-sized pieces.
2 Scald the gizzards and livers and rinse in cold water.
3 Soften the dried mushrooms in water, remove the stems and slice them thinly. Cut the bamboo shoots into flat pieces.
4 Slice the jellied potato-cake into 2¾″ × ¾″ × ¼″ thick pieces. Slit each piece down the center leaving the ends intact and twist one end through the slit.
5 Halve the green bell peppers, remove the seeds and cut them

into thick strips.
6 Fry the chicken giblets with the chopped garlic and ginger juice in a heated oiled pan. Then add the dried mushroom, jellied potato-cake and bamboo shoot, fry lightly

and season them with the soy sauce, sugar, salt and black pepper.
7 Dissolve the cornstarch powder in ⅓ cup broth. Add this starch liquid to the **#6** fried ingredients and bring to a boil to thicken.

1 Slit the outer part of the chicken gizzards.

3 Add the vegetables and fry lightly.

2 Scald the gizzards and livers in boiling water.

4 Add the starch liquid and boil until thick.

Spring Chicken Stew
Yonggyebokkŭm (영계볶음)

Ingredients   1¾ lb. whole spring chicken, ⅓ cup tiny soused, salted shrimp, 5 tbsp. chopped green onion, 1 tbsp. chopped garlic, 1 tbsp. ginger juice, 1 tbsp. sesame oil, 2 tbsp. sesame salt, black pepper, 5 red peppers, 5 green peppers, 1 round onion

Method   **1** Cut the chicken into 1⅔″ pieces, mix with the salted shrimp and seasoning and let stand.

2 Fry the seasoned chicken lightly in a pan. Pour in enough water to cover the chicken and simmer on low but steady heat.

3 Cut the round onion, red peppers and green peppers into ¼″ square pieces.

4 When the broth is almost evaporated, add the #3 vegetables and stir-fry briefly.

1 Cut the chicken into pieces.

4 Simmer #3 with the water.

2 Add the seasoning and salted shrimp to **#1** and let stand.

3 Fry the chicken pieces lightly in a fry pan.

5 Add the round onion and red pepper slices and fry.

38

Salted Beef in Soy Sauce
Soegogi Changjorim (쇠고기 장조림)

Ingredients   1⅓ lb. brisket of beef, 6 cups water, ¾ cup soy sauce, 3 tbsp. sugar, 20 quail eggs, 4 red peppers, 4 Korean green peppers, 20 cloves garlic

Method   **1** Cut the beef into 1⅔″×2″ pieces.
2 Boil the quail eggs for 7 minutes, rolling them so that the yolks will be centered, and peel.
3 Leave the stems on the peppers to a ⅓″ length.
4 Put enough water in a pan to cover the beef. Add the beef, bring to a hard boil and then simmer the beef on low heat.
5 When the meat is tender, add the garlic, soy sauce and sugar and simmer gently. Then add the **#2, #3** ingredients and bring to a boil.
6 Shred the beef and halve the peppers to serve.

Hint   You may use the shank of beef instead of the brisket of beef.

1 Cut the beef into 1⅔″×2″ pieces.

2 Boil the beef in the water.

3 Add the garlic, sugar and soy sauce and simmer.

4 Add the quail eggs and green peppers and boil briefly.

Potato and Beef in Soy Sauce
Soegogi Kamjajorim (쇠고기 감자조림)

Ingredients 1 oz. beef, green onion, garlic, sesame salt, 3 tbsp. soy sauce, 2 tbsp. sugar, ½ tbsp. sesame oil, pine nut powder, 2 potatoes, 1 cup water, Korean green peppers

Method **1** Cut the peeled potatoes into chestnut-sized pieces rounding the edges into smooth oval shapes and wash.
2 Mince the beef finely and season it with the green onion, garlic, sesame salt, soy sauce, sugar and sesame oil. Stir-fry the beef and potatoes, add water and boil.
3 When the potatoes are almost cooked, add the green peppers and simmer on high heat.

4 Place in a serving dish and sprinkle with the powdered pine nuts.
Hint   To make the seasoning sauce for this food: Combine ½ cup soy sauce, rice wine, 2 tbsp. sugar, water and black pepper.

1 Cut the potatoes into chestnut-sized pieces and round off the edges.

3 Add 1 cup water to the fried ingredients and bring to a boil.

2 Stri-fry the seasoned beef and potatoes.

4 When the liquid is almost evaporated, add the green peppers and simmer on high heat until nicely glazed.

Rolled Beef with Vegetables in Soy Sauce
Soegogi Yach'aemarijorim (쇠고기 야채말이조림)

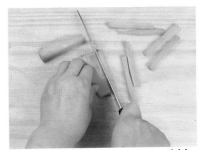

1 Cut the carrot into pencil-like pieces.

3 Wrap the vegetables in the beef slices and fasten.

5 Simmer the rolls on high heat until glazed.

2 Simmer the strips of burdock root with the seasoning.

4 Add the beef rolls to the boiling seasoning sauce.

Ingredients **A** ¼ lb. beef, 1 tsp. rice wine, 1½ tsp. sugar, 2 tsp. soy sauce, 2 tsp. red pepper paste, 1 knob ginger, 4 tbsp. water **B** ¼ burdock root, ¼ cup water, 1 tbsp. soy sauce, 1 tsp. sugar **C** ¼ carrot, 3 green peppers **D** ½ tomato, 5 lettuce leaves

Method **1** Cut the burdock root into pencil-like pieces. Scald and simmer with the **B** seasoning sauce.

2 Cut the carrot into the same size as the burdock root pieces and scald. Halve the green peppers to remove the seeds and cut them into thick strips.

3 Cut the beef into thin slices (about ⅛"). Wrap the green pepper, burdock root and carrot strips in the beef slice and fasten with a skewer. Simmer the A seasoning sauce until thick, add the beef rolls and cook them until the broth is almost evaporated.

4 Place the diagonally cut rolls on lettuce leaves on a plate and garnish with the tomato.

Hint Scalded Angelica shoots can be used instead of the green peppers.

Beef and Bamboo Shoot in Soy Sauce
Soegogi Chuksunjangjorim (쇠고기 죽순장조림)

1 Cut the bamboo shoot into 2″ long chunks.

2 Scrape out the cores of the bamboo shoot chunks.

3 Cover the insides with flour and stuff them with the seasoned beef.

Ingredients ½ lb. ground beef, 4 canned bamboo shoots, 1 tbsp. chopped green onion, 2 tsp. chopped garlic, 4 tbsp. flour, ½ tbsp. sesame salt, 1 tsp. sesame oil, 5 tbsp. soy sauce, 1 tbsp. sugar, ½ cup water, black pepper

Method 1 Mix the ground beef with the green onion, garlic, black pepper and sesame oil.
2 Cut the bamboo shoot into 2″ long chunks.
3 Scrape out the cores of the bam-
boo shoot chunks and dust the insides with flour.
4 Stuff the **#3** bamboo shoots with the beef mixture. Then dip the stuffed chunks in flour.
5 Boil the soy sauce, sugar and water in a pan. When the seasoning sauce boils, add the **#4** stuffed chunks and simmer gently until glazed. Sprinkle with the sesame oil.

Hint If fresh bamboo shoots (not canned) are used, scald them in boiling water to tenderize.

4 When the soy sauce, sugar and water boils, add the stuffed shoots and simmer until glazed.

42

Pork Meatballs in Soy Sauce
Twaejigogi Wanjajorim (돼지고기 완자조림)

Ingredients   **A** ¼ lb. pork, 1 tsp. salt, ginger juice, ¼ round onion, 2 tbsp. cornstarch powder
B 10 Korean green peppers, ¼ lb. cabbage, ¼ carrot, salad oil
C ⅓ cup water, 1 tbsp. red pepper paste, 1 tbsp. rice wine, 1 tsp. soy sauce, 1 tsp. sugar

Method   **1** Remove the stems from the long, Korean green peppers and cut them into ¾″ lengths.
2 Mince the pork finely and mix it with the chopped round onion, cornstarch powder, 1 tsp. salt and ginger juice. Shape the mixture into meatballs ¾″ in dia-meter. Roll the meatballs in cornstarch powder and deep-fry them in oil.
3 Bring the **C** seasoning to a boil, add the deep-fried meatballs and simmer. Then add the green peppers and cook briefly. Thread the meatballs and green peppers on skewers.
4 Arrange the skewered food around a centerpiece of cabbage strips and decorate the top with flower-shaped carrot pieces.

Hint   This dish can be served for guests, or as a side dish for lunch boxes or an hors d'oeuvre.

1 Chop the round onion finely.

3 Mix the meat with the seasoning and cornstarch powder.

5 Deep-fry the meatballs in oil.

2 Fry the chopped round onion.

4 Roll the meatballs in cornstarch powder.

6 When the seasoning boils, add and simmer the deep-fried meatballs.

Spareribs in Sweet Sauce
Twaejigalbi Kangjŏng (돼지갈비 강정)

Ingredients   1⅓ lb. pork ribs, black pepper, ginger juice, MSG, cornstarch powder, salad oil, 2 Korean green peppers, 2 red peppers, ¼ round onion, carrot, 2 cloves garlic, ¼ cup sweet sauce

Method   **1** Remove excess fat from the spareribs. Boil them and then score and marinate them in the seasoning.
2 Halve the red peppers and green peppers to remove the seeds. Cut the peppers, carrot and round onion into flat pieces and fry them lightly in an oiled pan.
3 Dip the spareribs in cornstarch powder and deep-fry them in oil.
4 Place the deep-fried ribs, vegetables and sweet sauce in a pan and simmer together on low heat.

Hint   **1** This is a high-grade dish which can be made easily for guests as a basic side dish if you prepare the sweet sauce beforehand.
2 To make the sweet sauce: 1 cup nicely aged soy sauce, ⅔ cup water, ½ lb. grain syrup (like dark corn syrup), 1 oz. ginger juice, ⅓ cup sugar, ¼ cup rice wine. Place the above ingredients in a pan and simmer them on low heat until thick.

Spareribs in Sweet Sauce

1 Remove excess fat from the spareribs and bring to a boil.

2 Slice the garlic, carrot and round onion into flat pieces.

4 Fry the vegetables lightly.

3 Dip the spareribs in cornstarch powder and deep-fry them in oil.

5 Add the sweet sauce and simmer.

44

Chicken in Soy Sauce
Takchorim (닭조림)

1 Cut the chicken into pieces.

2 Slice the carrot into large triangular pieces.

3 Fry the chicken pieces and remove the excess oil.

4 Add the seasoning sauce and water and simmer until glazed.

Ingredients   1 lb. chicken (half a chicken), 1 tbsp. oil, ½ carrot, 10 gingko nuts; 3 tbsp. soy sauce, 1½ tbsp. sugar, ginger juice, green onion, garlic, 1 cup water

Method   **1** Cut the chicken into pieces. Slice the carrot into large triangular pieces.

2 Fry the shelled gingko nuts in an oiled pan until they turn green.

3 Fry the carrot slightly. Fry the chicken pieces on high heat until golden brown.

4 Place the chicken, carrot, 1 cup water and half of the seasoning in a pan and simmer them on high heat for 10 minutes. When the liquid is almost evaporated, add the remaining seasoning and cook until glazed.

Deep-Fried Chicken in Soy Sauce
Takt'wigimjorim (닭튀김조림)

Ingredients   1 lb. chicken, 1 tbsp. rice wine, 1 tbsp. soy sauce, 1 green onion, 1 knob ginger, 1 cup cornstarch powder, ½ round onion, 2 Korean green peppers, ½ carrot, 2 cloves garlic, ⅓ cup sweet sauce, 2 oz. cabbage, ½ cucumber, 4 olive, tomato

Method   **1** Halve the whole chicken. Sprinkle the chicken with the rice wine and soy sauce and top it with the sliced ginger and round onion and steam it in a steamer.

2 Cut the steamed chicken into pieces. Dip them in flour and deep-fry them in oil.

3 Cut the round onion and green peppers into large pieces. Cut the carrot into crescent-shaped pieces and the garlic in flat pieces.

4 Fry the **#3** vegetables in an oiled pan. Add the chicken and sweet sauce and simmer until glazed.

5 Place the cabbage, cucumber and carrot cut into thin strips in a glassware dish and garnish with the olives and tomato. Serve this salad with the chicken.

Hint   To make the sweet sauce: Combine 1 cup nicely aged soy sauce, ½ lb. grain syrup (like dark corn syrup), ⅓ cup sugar, ⅔ cup water, 1 oz. ginger cut in flat pieces, ¼ cup rice wine, 1 tsp. black pepper, and MSG in a pan and simmer on low heat until thick.

1 Top the seasoned chicken with the sliced ginger and onion and steam.

3 Deep-fry the chicken pieces in oil until brown.

5 Fry the garlic and **#4** vegetables in an oiled pan.

2 Cut the steamed chicken into pieces and dip them in flour.

4 Slice the vegetables into big pieces.

6 Cook all the ingredients with the sweet sauce.

Broiled Foods
Deep-Fat Fried Foods

Barbecued Beef
Pulgogi (불고기)

Ingredients   1⅓ lb. top round or tenderloin of beef, 3 tbsp. sugar, 2 tbsp. rice wine, 5 tbsp. chopped green onion, 2 tbsp. chopped garlic, 6 tbsp. soy sauce, 1 tbsp. sesame salt, 2 tbsp. sesame oil, black pepper, MSG, lettuce, garland chrysanthemum, sesame leaves, garlic, small green onions

Method   **1** Slice the beef thinly and score lightly with a knife to make it more tender. Cut it into bite-sized pieces and marinate it in the sugar and rice wine.
2 Mix the marinated beef thoroughly with the soy sauce, chopped garlic, sesame salt, MSG and sesame oil.
3 Broil the seasoned beef over hot charcoal on a grill or in a fry pan. Pulgogi is delicious served with lettuce leaves, sesame leaves, garland chrysanthemum and garlic.

Hint   **1** Cut the beef against the grain to make it tender.
2 Pulgogi is generally broiled over charcoal on a grill at the table. Otherwise, you may use an oven-broiler heated to 570°F for 10 minutes.

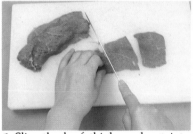

1 Slice the beef thinly and cut into bite-sized pieces.

2 Marinate the **#1** beef in the sugar and rice wine.

3 Add the seasoning sauce and mix well.

4 Broil the seasoned beef over hot charcoal.

Broil pulgogi over hot charcoal on a grill.

48

Broiled Beef Ribs
Soegalbigui (쇠갈비구이)

1 Score the meaty parts of the ribs taking care not to cut the bones.

2 Flatten the rib meat and score deeply.

Ingredients   4 lb. beef ribs, garlic, 6 tbsp. rice wine, 5 tbsp. sugar, 9 tbsp. chopped green onion, 3 tbsp. soy sauce, chopped garlic, 6 tbsp. sesame salt, 6 tbsp. sesame oil, lettuce leaves, green onion strips, round onion, pine nuts

Method   **1** Clean the ribs. Score the meaty parts of ribs taking care not to cut the bones. Flatten the rib meat, score deeply and place them in a bowl.

2 Sprinkle the ribs with the sugar

3 Add the seasoning sauce to the ribs and mix well.

and rice wine and mix well.

3 Mix the soy sauce with the chopped green onion, garlic, sesame salt and sesame oil to make the seasoning sauce.

4 Add the seasoning sauce to the **#2** ribs and let them stand for 1 hour.

5 Place the ribs on a hot grill and broil turning them several times.

4 Broil the ribs on a hot grill.

Broiled Beef Intestine in Salt
Kopch'ang Sogŭmgui (곱창 소금구이)

1 Remove excess fat from the small intestine with a scissors.

2 Cut the small intestine into 4″ lengths.

3 Clean the small intestine by rubbing it with salt.

4 Season the small intestine with the sesame oil, salt and black pepper.

Ingredients 1⅓ lb. small beef intestine, 2 tbsp. salt, 1 large green onion, 10 cloves garlic, 2 tbsp. sesame oil, black pepper, MSG, lettuce leaves, garland chrysanthemum, 2 red peppers

Method **1** Remove excess fat from the small intestine and cut it into 4″ lengths. Rub the small intestine with salt, wash and drain well.

2 Score the trimmed small intestine in various places.

3 Peel and clean the garlic. Cut the red peppers into small rings.

4 Season the small intestine with the sesame oil, black pepper, MSG and salt and mix well.

5 Place the small intestine pieces on a hot oiled grill and broil them evenly turning often.

6 Put the garlic cloves on the edge of a grill and cook gently.

7 When cooked, place the small intestine pieces on lettuce leaves on a plate and serve with the garlic, black pepper, salt, sesame salt and red pepper.

Hint Broil this food on high heat for top flavor. Otherwise, the meat juice is lost and the small intestine becomes hard too quickly.

Barbecued Pork
Twaejibulgogi (돼지불고기)

1 Sprinkle the pork with the ginger juice and mix well.

2 Add the seasoning sauce to **#1**, mix well and let it stand.

3 Brush the hot grill with sesame oil.

4 Broil the seasoned pork on the hot grill.

Ingredients 1⅓ lb. pork (with fat and skin remaining), 4 tbsp. soy sauce, 1 tbsp. salted soused shrimp, 3 tbsp. sugar, 1 tbsp. ginger juice, small green onion, 10 cloves garlic, 2 tbsp. sesame salt, 2 tbsp. sesame oil, black pepper, MSG, 3 green peppers

Method **1** Cut the pork into flat, thin pieces. Score finely, sprinkle it with the ginger juice and mix well.

2 Combine the soy sauce, salted soused shrimp, sugar, chopped garlic, chopped green onion, sesame salt, sesame oil, black pepper and MSG to make the seasoning sauce.

3 Mix the pork with the seasoning sauce and let it stand.

4 Place the seasoned pork pieces on a hot oiled grill and broil them turning often.

Hint Pork tastes best when cooked thoroughly.

Broiled Pork Spareribs
Twaejigalbigui (돼지갈비구이)

Ingredients   2⅔ lb. pork spareribs, 6 tbsp. soy sauce, black pepper, 4 tbsp. sugar, 6 tbsp. chopped green onion, 2 tbsp. chopped garlic, 1 tbsp. ginger juice, 2 tbsp. sesame salt, 2 tbsp. sesame oil, 2 Korean green peppers, 1 red pepper, 1 round onion, MSG, 6 skewers

Method   **1** Cut the spareribs into 2¾″ lengths and score them lightly at ⅓″ intervals. Sprinkle the ribs with the ginger juice, 2 tbsp. sugar and mix well.

2 Combine the soy sauce, sugar, chopped green onion, chopped garlic, sesame salt, sesame oil, black pepper and MSG to make the seasoning sauce.

3 Add the seasoning sauce to the ribs and rub it in with your hands, so that the ribs are well coated with the seasoning.

4 Place the spareribs on a hot oiled grill and broil them by turning often. Be careful so that the seasoning does not get scorched and fall off the ribs.

5 Serve the broiled spareribs topped with the sliced lemon.

Hint   Marinate the pork in the ginger juice and broil it basting with the seasoning sauce.

1 Cut the spareribs into 2¾″ lengths and score them at ⅓″ intervals.

2 Add the ginger juice and sugar and rub it in.

3 Sprinkle the **#2** ribs with the seasoning sauce and let them stand.

4 Broil the spareribs with the small green onion and garlic on a hot grill.

Hot Broiled Pork
Twaejigogi Koch'ujanggui (돼지고기 고추장구이)

Ingredients   1⅓ lb. pork, 2 tbsp. chopped garlic, 3 tbsp. chopped green onion, 4 tbsp. red pepper paste, 2 tbsp. sugar, 1 tbsp. sesame salt, 1 tbsp. sesame oil, 1 tbsp. ginger juice, black pepper, MSG, lettuce leaves, small green onion, sesame leaves, 10 cloves garlic

Method   **1** Use lean pork; slice it thinly and score it finely. Sprinkle the pork with the ginger juice and mix well.
2 Combine the red pepper paste, soy sauce, chopped green onion, garlic, sesame salt, sesame oil, sugar, black pepper and MSG to make the seasoned red pepper paste.
3 Add the seasoned red pepper paste to the meat and rub it in.
4 Place the seasoned meat on a hot grill and broil on medium heat.
5 Place the hot broiled meat on a plate and serve with the lettuce leaves, sesame leaves, small green onion, garlic and stuffed cucumber kimchi.
Hint   Sprinkling the pork with ginger juice removes any odor; broil for a tasty dish.

1 Slice the pork thinly.

2 Score the sliced pork lightly.

3 Add the ginger juice to **#2.**

4 Add the seasoned red pepper paste to the meat and rub it in.

5 Oil the grill.

6 Broil the meat on direct heat first and then cook on medium heat.

Baked Whole Chicken
T'ongdakkui (통닭구이)

1 Sprinkle the clean chicken with the salt, black pepper and ginger juice.

3 Turn the wings backward and twist the legs.

4 Layer the vegetables in the bottom, then put the chicken on them and put the remaining vegetables on top.

2 Cut the rear part of the neck and fasten it in the back of the chicken with a toothpick.

5 Bake the chicken for 40 minutes.

Ingredients   1 whole chicken, 1 tsp. salt, ¾ oz. butter, 1 round onion, ½ carrot, ½ cup sweet soy sauce, 1 knob ginger, parsley, 1 tomato, ribbon

Method   **1** Clean the whole chicken and sprinkle it with the salt, black pepper and ginger juice.
2 Cut the round onion and carrot into thin strips. Layer half of the vegetables on the bottom of the oven pan, then place the chicken on these vegetables and layer the remaining vegetables on top of the chicken.
3 Bake the chicken for 10 minutes in an oven.
4 Remove the vegetables from the chicken and bake for 10 minutes more. Then baste it with the sweet soy sauce and bake it for 20 minutes more.
5 Wrap the legs of the chicken with foil and tie the ribbon on the neck. Garnish with the tomato and parsley.

Deep-Fried Beef
Soegogit'wigim (쇠고기튀김)

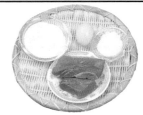

Ingredients   1 lb. beef, 1 cup cornstarch powder, 1 egg, salad oil, black pepper, MSG, 2 oz. Chinese noodles, 1 tsp. salt, parsley

Method   **1** Trim the lean beef and slice it thinly.

2 Cut the sliced beef into bite-sized pieces. Mix the beef pieces with the salt, black pepper, MSG and beaten egg well and dip them in cornstarch powder.

3 Heat the oil in a deep-fry pan and when smoking, add the meat pieces and deep-fry them until golden brown; after few minutes fry them once more.

4 Deep-fry the Chinese noodles and spread them on a plate. Serve the deep-fried beef with kimchi and garnish with the parsley.

Hint   When you deep-fry the beef, do not put too many beef pieces in the hot oil. The oil temperature falls if you add too many at a time.

1 Cut the sliced beef into bite-sized pieces.

3 Dip the seasoned meat in the cornstarch powder.

4 Deep-fry the beef pieces twice.

2 Mix the beef with the salt, black pepper, MSG and beaten egg.

Deep-Fried Beef and Gingko Nuts
Soegogi Samsaegunhaengt'wigim (쇠고기 삼색은행튀김)

Ingredients   ²⁄₃ lb. beef, ½ cup gingko nuts, 2 round onions, 1 carrot, 5 green peppers, 1 tbsp. salt, ½ cup cornstarch powder, black pepper, MSG, 10 skewers, parsley

Method   **1** Choose tender, lean beef and cut it into ½" square pieces. Score finely and sprinkle with salt and black pepper.
2 Cut the carrot and round onions into the same size as the beef pieces.
3 Fry the shelled gingko nuts until green and peel off the top-skin.
4 Halve the green peppers to remove the seeds and cut them into ½" square pieces.

5 Season the above ingredients with salt, black pepper and MSG.
6 Skewer the beef, carrot, round onion, green pepper pieces and ginko nuts alternating the colors.
7 Sprinkle the cornstarch powder over the skewered food.
8 Heat the oil to 360°F in a pan and deep-fry two or three skewers of food at a time. Deep-fry them once again after a few minutes.
9 Drain on absorbent paper, place the deep-fried food on a plate and garnish with the parsley.

1 Cut the round onions, carrot and green   peppers into ½" square pieces.

3 Skewer the prepared ingredients.

4 Sprinkle the constarch powder over the skewered food.

2 Stir-fry the gingko nuts and remove the inner skin.

5 Deep-fry the skewered food in oil.

Deep-Fried Beef Rolled in Sesame Leaves
Soegogi Kkaennipmarit'wigim (쇠고기 깻잎말이튀김)

1 Mix and season the mashed bean curd and minced beef.

4 Stick the skewers into the rolls to fasten.

2 Clean the sesame leaves and dry off the moisture. Then dip the insides into flour.

5 Dip the rolls into flour and then into beaten egg and deep-fry them in boiling oil.

3 Place a spoonful of the meat mixture on a sesame leaf and roll it up.

Ingredients   ⅔ lb. beef, 10 sesame leaves, ½ cake bean curd, 1 egg, ½ cup flour, 2 tbsp. chopped green onion, 1 tbsp. chopped garlic, 2 tsp. sesame salt, 2 tsp. sesame oil, 1 tbsp. salt, black pepper, MSG, 10 small skewers, ½ cucumber, 2 bundles parsley, 1 red radish

Method   **1** Slice the beef thinly and mince well.

2 Wrap the bean curd in a clean cloth, squeeze out the excess water and mash it finely.

3 Combine the meat, bean curd, chopped green onion, garlic, sesame salt, sesame oil, black pepper, MSG and salt and mix well.

4 Wash the sesame leaves and dry off the moisture.

5 Dip the insides of sesame leaves in flour. Place the spoonful of the meat mixture on each leaf and roll it up and fasten with a small skewer.

6 Dip the rolls into flour and then into beaten egg and deep-fry them in boiling oil.

7 Drain and arrange the cucumber cut into thin rings and diagonally cut rolls in the center of a plate. Garnish with the parsley and red radish.

Hint   Deep-fry the food in very hot oil until crisp. To drain stand the deep-fried food on end, so that it does not become soft.

Deep-Fried Chicken Legs
Taktarit'wigim (닭다리튀김)

Ingredients   6 chicken legs, 1 tbsp. ginger juice, ½ tbsp. salt, 1 egg, ½ cup cornstarch powder, black pepper, MSG, frying oil, parsley, red radish

Method   **1** Loosen the meat from the bones being careful to leave it attached at the lower end. Score the meat to tenderize and sprinkle it with the ginger juice, black pepper, MSG and salt rubbing the seasonings in.

2 Pour the beaten egg evenly over the meat.

3 Dip the chicken legs into the cornstarch powder and deep-fry them twice in boiling oil.

4 Place the deep-fried chicken legs on a plate and garnish with the parsley and red radish.

Hint   Place the cucumber, carrot, cabbage and boiled egg white cut into thin strips in a bowl and sprinkle the sieved egg yolk on top. Serve the deep-fried chicken legs with these vegetables.

1 Loosen the meat from the bones, leaving the lower ends attached.

2 Sprinkle with the salt, ginger juice and black pepper and mix well.

3 Pour the beaten egg evenly over the meat.

4 Dip the legs into the cornstarch powder and deep-fry them in oil.

Pan-Fried Foods
Skewered Foods

Fried Pork in Egg Batter
Tonjŏn (돈전)

1 Wrap the bean curd in a cloth, squeeze out the water and mash it.

2 Mix the minced pork, kimchi and bean curd with the seasoning well.

3 Oil your hands and shape the mixture into round, flat patties.

Ingredients ½ lb. ground pork, 1 cake bean curd, ½ cup flour, 2 cloves garlic, 1 large green onion, ¼ lb. kimchi, parsley, sesame oil, 2 eggs, salt, black pepper, MSG, 1 tsp. ginger juice

Method 1 Wrap the bean curd in a cloth, squeeze out the water and mash it.

2 Squeeze out the water from the kimchi. Chop the kimchi and green onion finely.

3 Mix the #1, #2 ingredients, ground pork, garlic, salt, black pepper, sesame oil and MSG and shape the mixture into round, flat patties.

4 Dip the patties into flour, then into beaten egg and fry them until golden brown. Garnish with the parsley and green onion cut into thin strips.

Hint 1 Season the kimchi and bean curd and mix them thoroughly with a flat wooden spoon or with your hands so that the patties will be nicely shaped. You may use parboiled mung bean sprouts instead of the kimchi. When draining the fried food in a wicker tray, make only one layer.

2 Be sure to remove all the fat from the pork as it may otherwise be too greasy. Also, cook the pork well.

60

Fried Liver in Egg Batter
Kanjŏn (간전)

Ingredients ⅔ lb. liver, 1 egg, ½ cup flour, salt, black pepper, lemon, olive

Method **1** Remove the membrane from the liver and rinse to remove any blood.
2 Slice the liver thinly and score and sprinkle it with the salt and black pepper.
3 Dip the liver into flour and then into beaten egg.
4 Fry the liver in a moderately hot oiled pan until golden brown and garnish with the lemon and olive.

Hint **1** Soak the liver in water to remove any blood; otherwise the fried liver becomes black.
2 Score the liver; otherwise the fried liver will curl up.

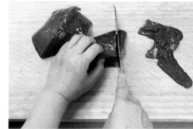

1 Remove the membrane from the liver and rinse it to remove any blood.

2 Slice the liver and score it lightly.

3 Sprinkle the liver slices with the salt and black pepper.

4 Dip the liver slices into flour and then into beaten egg and fry them until golden brown.

Skewered Beef
Soegogi Sanjŏk (쇠고기 산적)

1 Cut the beef into 3″ long and ¼″ thick strips.

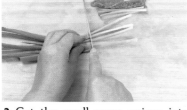

2 Cut the small green onions into lengths shorter than the meat strips.

3 Marinate the meat in the seasoning sauce.

4 String the meat and small green onion strips alternately on skewers.

A grill may be used for broiling the skewered food.

5 Fry the skewered food in an oiled pan.

Ingredients   ½ lb. beef, ¼ lb. small green onion, seasoning sauce: (1 tbsp. sugar, 2 tsp. rice wine, 2 tbsp. soy sauce, 2 large green onions, 3 cloves garlic, 1 tbsp. sesame salt, 2 tsp. sesame oil), salad oil

Method   **1** Select lean beef and cut it into thin slices about ¼″ thick.
2 Score the beef slices to tenderize and cut them into 3″ long, pencil-wide strips.
3 Trim the small green onions and cut them into lengths slightly shorter than the beef strips.
4 Marinate the beef in the seasoning sauce.
5 Trim the wooden or bamboo skewers with a knife and rinse them in water.
6 String the seasoned meat and small green onion strips alternately on skewers and beginning and ending with the meat. Then baste the filled skewers with the seasoning sauce.
7 Fry the skewered food in a hot oiled pan until the meat is browned on both sides.
Hint   **1** Cut the meat into strips longer than the vegetables, as the meat shrinks when cooked.
2 When you string the food on skewers, stick the skewers into the upper part of the food.

Skewered Pork and Kimchi
Twaejigogi Kimch'isanjök (돼지고기 김치산적)

1 Cut the pork into ⅓"×3½" strips and pound them with the back of knife.

2 Season the pork with the ginger, garlic, soy sauce, sugar and green onions.

3 Squeeze out the water from the kimchi and season.

Ingredients   ½ lb. pork, ½ lb. kimchi, 1 tbsp. sugar, 2 tsp. sessame oil, 10 small green onions, ½ cup flour, 1 egg, various seasonings, parsley, red radish

Method   **1** Cut the pork into ⅓"×3½" strips and pound the pork strips with the back of knife to tenderize them. Marinate them in the seasoning sauce.
2 Cut the kimchi into 3" lengths and squeeze out the water. Season it with the sesame oil and sugar.
3 Cut the small green onions into 3" lengths.
4 String the pork, kimchi and green onion strips alternately on skewers. Dip one side of the skewered food into flour.
5 Dip the #4 skewered food into beaten egg and fry it until golden brown.
6 Garnish with the parsley and red radish and serve with the seasoning sauce for dipping.

Hint   A tasty variation is angelica shoots instead of kimchi.

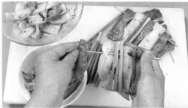

4 String the pork, kimchi, and small green onions alternately on skewers.

5 Dip one side of the #4 skewered food into flour.

6 Dip the skewered food into beaten egg and fry.

Broiled Chicken Patty
Takkogi Sopsanjŏk (닭고기 섭산적)

Ingredients   1 spring chicken, 4 tbsp. chopped green onion, 2 tbsp. chopped garlic, 1 tbsp. chopped ginger, 1 tbsp. sesame salt, 2 tbsp. sesame oil, ½ tsp. salt, 3 tbsp. soy sauce, black pepper, red pepper thread, lettuce, cucumber

Method   **1** Remove the meat from the bones and mince it finely.
2 Add the seasoning sauce to the minced meat and mix well. Shape the mixture into round flat patties.
3 Broil the patties in a hot oiled pan or on a grill, taking care not to burn them. (Or, you may fry them in an oiled pan on medium heat.)
Hint   Mince all the ingredients finely and mix them thoroughly,

so that the patties keep a nice shape. This dish is especially good for students' lunch boxes.

1 Remove the meat from the bones and mince it finely.

3 Shape the **#2** mixture into round flat patties on an oiled kitchen board.

2 Add the seasoning sauce and mix well.

4 Pan-broil the patties until brown.

Skewered Beef with Vegetables
Chapsanjŏk (잡산적)

Ingredients   ¼ lb. beef, ¼ lb. bellflower roots, 10 small green onions, 2 oz. bracken (fern shoots), ½ carrot, 5 dried brown, oak mushrooms, seasoning sauce: (3 tbsp. soy sauce, 1 tsp. sesame salt, 1 tbsp. green onion, ½ tbsp. garlic, sesame oil, black pepper, MSG), skewers

Method   1 Cut the beef into thin slices about ¼″ thick. Score the slices evenly and cut them into ⅓″ × 3″ strips.
2 Soak the bellflower roots to remove the bitterness. Scald in boiling water, cut into 2¾″ long pencil-wide strips and pound them with the back of knife to tenderize.
3 Trim the small green onions and dried mushrooms and cut them into 2¾″ long strips.
4 Cut the bracken and carrot into 2¾″ long pencil-wide strips and scald them slightly.
5 Make the seasoning sauce.
6 Marinate the beef in one-third of the seasoning sauce for 20 minutes.
7 Mix the carrot, bracken, small green onion and bellflower roots with the seasoning sauce.
8 String the above ingredients on skewers alternating the colors and fry them in a fry pan.

1 Cut the beef into ¼″ thick and ⅓″ × 3″ strips.

2 Cut the carrot, dried mushrooms, bracken and bellflower roots into 2¾″ long pencil-wide strips.

3 Mix the beef and vegetables with the seasoning sauce.

4 Skewer the ingredients alternating the colors and fry

Skewered Boiled Beef
Hwayangjŏk (화양적)

Ingredients ⅓ lb. pressed meat, 6 dried brown, oak mushrooms, 5 bellflower roots, 1 cucumber, 2 carrots, 2 eggs, 1 tbsp. chopped pine nuts, ½ tbsp. sesame salt, 1 tsp. sesame oil, 1 tbsp. chopped green onion, 1 tbsp. chopped garlic, ½ tbsp. sugar, black pepper, red radish, 2 tbsp. soy sauce

Method **1** To make the pressed meat: Boil the beef or the pork. Wrap the boiled meat in a cloth and press it with a heavy weight. When the meat is cooled, slice it into strips 2⅓" long and ¼" thick. **2** Soak the dried mushrooms in water and remove the stems. Slice them into 2⅓" lengths.

3 Shred the bellflower roots into strips ¼" thick. Cut the carrot into strips 2⅓" long and ¼" thick. Scald them in boiling water.

4 Choose a thin, tender cucumber and cut it into strips 2⅓" long and

¼″ thick. Sprinkle with salt.

5 Separate the whites and yolks of eggs and beat gently. Mix the beaten egg whites, and also the yolks with 1 tbsp. cornstarch flour, 1 tbsp. water and salt each. Fry these mixtures in a square pan in thick sheets and let them cool. Cut the egg sheets into strips 2⅓″ long.

6 Season all the ingredients except the egg strips with the soy sauce, sesame salt, black pepper, sesame oil, green onion and chopped garlic and fry lightly.

7 String the ingredients on skewers alternating the colors. Sprinkle the top with powdered pine nuts on a plate. Garnish with red radish and parsley.

Hint Bellflower root is a tasty addition to this dish. It is an alkaline food containing sugar, fiber, calcium and iron.

1 Cut the pressed meat into strips ⅓″ × 2⅓″.

2 Cut the vegetables into the same size strips as the meat.

3 Season and fry the **#1** meat and **#2** vegetable strips lightly.

4 Skewer the ingredients alternating the colors.

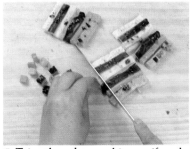

5 Trim the edges making uniformly sized servings.

Skewered Rice Cake
Ttoksanjŏk (떡산적)

Ingredients 3 rolls of rice cake, ⅓ lb. beef, 1 carrot, 10 small green onions, 6 dried brown, oak mushrooms, 3 tbsp. soy sauce, 2 large green onions, 3 cloves garlic, 1 tbsp. sesame oil, 2 tbsp. sesame salt, 2 tsp. sugar, black pepper, red pepper threads, 10 skewers

Method 1 Cut the rolls of rice cake into 2¾″ lengths and quarter them lengthwise. Scald and rinse in cold water.

2 Score the beef lightly and cut it into 3″ long, pencil-wide strips.

3 Cut the carrot into 2¾″ long, pencil-wide strips and scald them in boiling water.

4 Trim and cut the small green onions into 2¾″ lengths.

5 Soak the dried mushrooms, remove the stems and cut the mushrooms into ⅓″ wide, 2¾″ long strips.

6 Chop the green onions and garlic finely.

7 Combine the soy sauce, green onion, garlic, sesame oil, sesame salt, black pepper and sugar to make the seasoning sauce.

8 Mix the prepared ingredients with half of the seasoning sauce.

9 String the seasoned ingredients on skewers alternating the colors beginning and ending with the rice cakes.

10 Baste both sides of the skewered food with the remaining seasoning sauce and fry them in an oiled pan or broil them on a grill.

Hint 1 When the rice cake hardens a little, you can cut it into pretty shapes. If the rice cake becomes too hard, cut it and then scald and rinse in cold water before frying.

2 Trim both edges of the skewered food, so that it looks neat.

1 Cut the rolls of rice cake into 2¾″ lengths and quarter them

2 Scald the rice cake in boiling water and rinse in cold water.

3 Fry the skewered food basting with the seasoning sauce.

68

Raw Meats
Pressed Meats

Raw Meat
Yuk'oe (육회)

Ingredients ⅔ lb. beef, 2½ tbsp. soy sauce, 1½ tbsp. sugar, 1 tbsp. chopped green onion, 2 tsp. chopped garlic, 1 tbsp. sesame salt, 2 tbsp. sesame oil, 1 crisp Korean pear, 2 tbsp. pine nut powder, 4 lettuce leaves, 1 egg yolk

Method **1** Select fresh, lean beef. Slice thinly and cut again into thin strips; mix with the seasoning sauce.
2 Peel the Korean pear and cut it into thin strips. Soak it in sugar water for a while and drain.
3 Heap the beef strips on the lettuce leaves in the center of the plate with the pear strips on the side.
4 Put the egg yolk on top of the meat and sprinkle it with powdered pine nuts.

Hint You must use only very fresh beef of good quality because it is being eaten raw.

1 Slice the beef thinly and cut it into thin strips.

4 Soak the pear in sugar water and drain.

2 Mix the beef strips with the seasoning sauce.

5 Place the pear and beef strips on the lettuce leaves.

3 Peel the pear and cut it into thin strips.

6 Put the egg yolk on top of the beef.

Sliced Raw Liver and Tripe
Kan · Ch'ŏnyŏp'oe (간 · 처녑회)

Ingredients ½ lb. liver, ⅔ lb. tripe, 5 tbsp. pine nuts, 3 tbsp. sesame oil, 1 tbsp. salt, black pepper, sesame salt, lettuce leaves

Method 1 Remove the membrane from the liver and slice it thinly. Then rub it lightly with salt and rinse it in running water to remove any blood.

2 Rub half of the tripe with salt and rinse it in water. Parboil in boiling water, rinse it in cold water and remove the skin.

3 Rub the remaining tripe with salt and clean it to remove the scent.

4 Cut the liver and tripe into ¾″ wide and 2″ long slices. Put a pine nut on each slice and roll it up.

5 Arrange the liver and tripe rolls on lettuce leaves on a plate.

6 Serve with sesame oil, black pepper, sesame salt and salt.

Hint 1 Though you can eat raw tripe, it is safer to eat slightly scalded tripe.

2 Scald the tripe only briefly for easier removal of the skin.

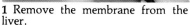

1 Remove the membrane from the liver.

2 Rub the tripe with salt and rinse it to remove the scent.

3 Scald half of the tripe in boiling water and skin it.

4 Put a pine nut at the end of each slice of liver and tripe and roll firmly.

Cold Cooked Chicken and Vegetables
Takkogi Naengch'ae (닭고기 냉채)

Ingredients   1 lb. chicken, ½ lb. jellyfish, 1 carrot, 1 cucumber, 1 pear, 2 eggs, mustard sauce: (7 tbsp. mustard powder, 3 tbsp. sugar, 2 tbsp. salt, 1 tbsp. soy sauce, ½ cup water, ½ cup vinegar), chopped stone mushrooms

Method   1 Clean the chicken well and baste it with the soy sauce. Deep-fry the chicken in oil and cut the meat into thick strips.
2 Separate the egg yolk and egg white. Fry the yolk into a thin sheet. Mix the egg white with the chopped stone mushrooms and fry in a thin sheet.
3 Cut the egg sheets, carrot and cucumber into flat rectangles.

4 Scald the jellyfish briefly in warm water (140° F). Then cut it into 2⅓" long strips and mix it with the sugar and vinegar.
5 Cut one-third of the prepared cucumber pieces into thin strips.
6 Arrange the flat pieces of carrot, cucumber, egg white and egg yolk around the edge of a plate. Pile the sliced chicken in the center and ring it with the jellyfish and cucumber strips.
7 Serve with ½ cup of the mustard sauce.

Hint   If you fry the chicken basted with the soy sauce, the color becomes a lovely brown, but if you steam the chicken instead, it tastes especially delicious.

1 Cut the fried chicken into thick strips.

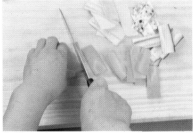

2 Cut the carrot, egg sheets and cucumber into flat pieces.

3 Mix the jellyfish strips with the vinegar and sugar.

Pressed Boiled Beef
Soegogisat'ae P'yŏnyuk (쇠고기사태 편육)

Ingredients **A** 1⅓ lb. shank of beef, ½ round onion, ½ carrot, lettuce leaves

B 5 tbsp. soy sauce, 2 tbsp. vinegar, 2 tbsp. chopped green onion, 1 tbsp. chopped garlic, 1 tsp. sugar, black pepper, sesame salt

Method **1** Clean the shank of beef.

2 Cut the round onion and carrot into thin strips.

3 Boil the shank of beef with the round onion and carrot.

4 Take the meat out of the pot and wrap it in a cloth and press it with a heavy weight.

5 When the meat becomes firm, cut it into thin slices. Arrange the sliced meat on lettuce leaves on a plate.

6 Make the seasoning sauce with the **B** ingredients and serve. .

1 Cut the round onion and carrot into thin strips.

3 When the meat is well-done, drain it and wrap it in a cloth.

2 Boil the shank of beef and **#1** vegetables.

4 Press the meat with a heavy weight.

Pressed Boiled Pork
Twaejigogi P'yŏnyuk (돼지고기 편육)

Ingredients 1⅓ lb. pork, 2 tbsp. soybean paste, 2 knobs ginger, ½ lb. kimchi, tiny soused salted shrimp seasoning: (4 tbsp. salted shrimp juice, 2 tbsp. chopped green onion, 1 tsp. chopped garlic, sesame salt, 1 tbsp. red pepper powder, black pepper, sesame oil, water), lettuce leaves

Method 1 Wash the pork in cold water, cut it into large pieces and tie them together tightly with string.
2 Slice the ginger thinly.
3 Dissolve and boil the soybean paste in water. Add the meat and ginger when boiling and simmer until tender.
4 Remove the excess fat and froth which have floated to the top.
5 When the meat is well-done, drain and rinse in cold water, wrap in a cloth and press it with a heavy weight.
6 When the meat becomes firm, cut it into thin slices. Arrange the sliced meat on lettuce leaves on a plate and serve with the kimchi.
7 Mix the salted shrimps with the seasoning and serve. Add some water if the soused shrimp is too salty.

Hint Pressed boiled pork is very tasty served with garland chrysanthemum, green pepper or vinegar-red pepper sauce.

1 Boil the pork and sliced ginger.

2 Remove excess fat and froth from the top.

3 Wrap the meat in a cloth and press it with a heavy weight.

4 Add the seasoning to the tiny soused salted shrimp.

Fish
Shellfish
Vegetables

Soups
Boiled Main Dishes
Stews
Simmered Mixed Dishes

Clear Fish Soup
Chogi Malgŭnjangkuk (조기 맑은 장국)

Ingredients 1 yellow corvina, 2 oz. beef, 1½ tbsp. soy sauce, ½ tbsp. chopped garlic, ½ tsp. sesame oil, black pepper, 3½ cup water, 1 egg, garland chrysanthemum, 3 small green onions

Method 1 Buy yellow corvina and cut it into several large pieces. 2 Slice the beef cutting against the grain. Season and fry it. Simmer the fried beef with the water to make the meat broth. 3 When the broth boils, add the corvina pieces and bring to a boil again. 4 When the corvina is cooked, check the seasoning and add the sliced small green onion and beaten egg. Add the leaves of garland chrysanthemum just before serving.

Hint Use chopsticks to hold back the beaten egg so you can pour it slowly into the broth.

1 Cut the corvina into pieces.

2 Boil the beef and then add the corvina.

3 When the corvina is cooked, season and slowly add the beaten egg.

Cold Seaweed and Cucumber Soup
Miyŏk Oinaengkuk (미역 오이냉국)

Ingredients ¼ lb. cucumber, ½ strip brown seaweed, 1½ cup water, 1 tsp. vinegar, 1 tsp. sugar, 1 tsp. soy sauce, 2 tsp. salt, ⅓ green onion, 1 red pepper, ice, MSG

Method **1** Cut the cucumber into thin strips.
2 Soak and clean the seaweed in water. Scald slightly in boiling water and rinse it in cold water. Cut it at ⅓″ intervals.
3 Pour the water into a bowl and sprinkle in the vinegar, sugar and salt. Add the cucumber, seaweed, red pepper strips and ice and serve.

Hint **1** If you add thinly sliced tomato, it becomes "cold tomato soup".
2 Be sure to boil the water first and then use it after it is cooled.

1 Cut the cucumber into thin strips.

3 Season the water with the vinegar, sugar and salt.

2 Scald the soaked seaweed in boiling water and cut.

4 Add the #1 and #2 ingredients to #3.

Croaker Pepper-Pot Soup
Minŏ Maeunťang (민어 매운탕)

1 Scale the croaker and cut it into several large pieces.

2 Cut the carrot and radish into flower-like shapes.

3 When the soup boils, add the fish pieces.

Ingredients 1 croaker, ¼ lb. beef, 1 zucchini, 2 tbsp. red pepper paste, 1 tsp. sesame oil, 1 tsp. red pepper powder, 2 cloves garlic, black pepper, sesame salt, 10 sea mussels, red pepper, green pepper, 3 cups rice water, green onion, 1 piece radish, 1 piece carrot

Method 1 Cut the croaker into several large pieces.
2 Slice the beef thinly and pound it with the back of the knife to tenderize. Season it with the red pepper paste, sesame oil, red pepper powder, garlic, black pepper and sesame salt.
3 Wash the sea mussels in salt water. Cut the zucchini, green pepper and red pepper into large pieces.
4 Stir-fry the seasoned beef and squash in a pan, add the rice water and bring to a boil.
5 When the soup boils, add the fish, flower-shaped carrot and radish pieces and boil again. Then add the sea mussels, green pepper, red pepper, and green onion and bring to a boil once more.

Hint 1 You may use corvina or pollack instead of the croaker according to the season.
2 Croaker tastes better in summer during the breeding season and it may be used then for raw fish or fried fish dishes.

4 When the soup boils again, add the remaining ingredients.

Bellflower Root Soup
Saengch'ot'ang (생초탕)

Ingredients   3 oz. ground beef, ¼ lb. bellflower roots, various seasoning, 2 oz. beef, 1 round onion, 3 dried brown, oak mushrooms, 2 eggs, ½ bundle garland chrysanthemum, 1 tbsp. flour, 1 tbsp. red pepper paste, 2 tsp. salt, 3 cups water, 1 tsp. chopped green onion, 1 tsp. chopped garlic, sesame salt, sesame oil, 1 red pepper, MSG

Method   **1** Trim the bellflower roots and rub them well with salt.

2 Wash the bellflower roots and drain. Shred thinly and chop a little.

3 Mix the bellflower roots and ground beef with the flour and beaten egg and season.

4 Slice 2 oz. of beef in flat pieces, season and fry. Then add the sliced dried mushrooms, round onion, and water to this beef and bring it all to a boil.

5 Shape the **#3** mixture into meatballs 1¼″ in diameter. Dip them into the beaten egg and drop them into the **#4** boiling soup.

6 When the meatballs have risen to the top, add sliced red pepper or leaves of garland chrysanthemum.

Hint   You may add some more red pepper paste to the hot soup.

3 Fry the beef pieces and then add the sliced round onion, dried mushrooms and water and boil.

4 When the soup boils, add the meatballs dipped into the beaten egg.

1 Trim the bellflower roots and shred them finely using a toothpick.

2 Mix the ground beef and bellflower roots with the flour and beaten egg and season.

Hot Pollack Soup
Tongt'aetchigae (동태찌개)

Ingredients 2 pollack, ¼ lb. beef, ½ zucchini, 2 tbsp. red pepper paste, 2 cloves garlic, 3 cups rice water, 4 dried brown, oak mushrooms, 1 large green onion, 3 leaves of garland chrysanthemum, ½ cake bean curd, red pepper, green pepper, ¼ lb. clam, 1 tbsp. soy sauce, 1 tsp. sesame oil, sesame salt

Method　**1** Trim the pollack and cut it into three or four pieces.
2 Cut the zucchini into half-circles. Cut the red peppers, green peppers and large green onion diagonally.
3 Soak the dried mushrooms in water and slice. Cut the bean curd into bite-sized squares.
4 Slice the beef in flat pieces cutting against the grain. Mix the beef, dried mushrooms and zucchini slices with the soy sauce, red pepper paste, sesame salt, garlic and sesame oil. Then fry the mixture lightly in a pot, add the rice water and boil.
5 When the beef broth is fully flavored, add the ground red pepper to the soup.
6 When the soup boils, add the pollack, large green onion and green pepper and bring to a boil again.
7 Add the clams and bean curd pieces to the soup and boil. Add the garland chrysanthemum just before taking the pot off the fire.
Hint　In this simmered dish it is customary to add the clams after the other ingredients are cooked.

1 Trim the pollack and cut it into three or four pieces.

2 Slice the beef and fry it with the seasonings.

3 Add the rice water to **#2** and boil. Then add the zucchini, dried mushroom and ground red pepper.

4 Add the pollack to **#3** and boil. Last of all add the clams and bean curd pieces and boil once more.

Crab Pot-Stew
Kkotketchigae (꽃게찌개)

Ingredients　3 red crabs, ⅓ lb. beef, 1 cake bean curd, 1 egg, 1 large green onion, 1 tsp. sesame oil, 2 tbsp. chopped green onion, 1 tbsp. chopped garlic, salt, black pepper, 1 tbsp. red pepper paste, 1 tbsp. soybean paste, 1 tbsp. red pepper powder, 1 red pepper

Method　**1** Scrub the crabs clean with a brush.
2 Open the crabs by splitting them between the top and bottom shell. Cut off the legs and remove all the crab meat with a spoon.
3 Season the crab meat, minced beef and mashed bean curd with the sesame oil, green onion, chopped garlic, salt and black pepper. Add the beaten egg.
4 Dip the top shell of the crab into flour and stuff it with the **#3** mixture. Dip the stuffed crab shell into flour and then into beaten egg and fry lightly in a fry pan.
5 Slice the large green onion diagonally. Dissolve the red pepper paste, soybean paste and red pepper powder in water in a pot and bring to a boil. When it boils, add the crab, large green onion, chopped green onion, red pepper and garlic and check the seasoning.

1 Remove the crab meat from the crab shell.

2 Mix the crab meat, bean curd and beef together.

3 Stuff the top shell of the crab with the **#2** mixture.

4 Fry the stuffed crab shell lightly in a fry pan.

5 When the broth boils, add the fried crab and boil again.

Spicy Dried Pollack Stew
Pugŏ Koch'ujangtchigae 〈북어 고추장찌개〉

Ingredients   2 dried pollack, ⅓ lb. bean sprouts, 3 tbsp. red pepper paste, green onion, garlic, 2 green peppers, 2 red peppers, 1 tsp. salt, 3 cup water

Method   **1** Pound and soak the dried pollack in water until tender. Remove the flesh from the bones and cut it into pieces 2″ long.

2 Dissolve the red pepper paste in the water, add the dried pollack pieces and bring to a boil.

3 Add the trimmed bean sprouts, chopped garlic and sliced green onion and season them with salt.

4 Top the soup with the red pepper and green pepper cut into rings.

Hint   Simmer the softened dried pollack until tender. Then add the bean sprouts.

1 Cut the softened pollack into pieces 2″ long.

3 When the dried pollack becomes soft, add the trimmed bean sprouts.

2 Add the dried pollack pieces to the boiling broth.

4 Add the sliced green onion and season the soup with salt.

Red Snapper Hot Pot
Tomi Chŏn-gol (도미 전골)

Ingredients 1 red snapper, ⅓ lb. beef, 2 large green onions, 2 oz. radish, ½ carrot, ½ bundle watercress, ½ bundle garland chrysanthemum, 20 gingko nuts, 1 red pepper, ½ round onion, 6 dried brown, oak mushrooms, 1 oz. konyak: jellied potato-cake, salt, black pepper, MSG, 3 cups meat stock, 3 tbsp. soy sauce, 1 tbsp. garlic, 1 tbsp. sesame salt, 2 tbsp. cornstarch powder, black pepper

Method 1 Scale the red snapper and remove the entrails through the gills. Clean and make diagonal slits on the red snapper.
2 Sprinkle the salt and black pepper in the slits. Dust the slits with cornstarch powder.
3 Mix the beef, round onion, red pepper, green onion and chopped garlic with the seasoning. Stuff the slits with this mixture.
4 Soak the dried mushrooms in water until soft, remove the stems and cut them into large pieces.
5 Halve the radish trimming the edges into a flower-petal design. Cut the carrot into flowerlike shapes and the watercress into 2⅓" lengths.
6 Cut the jellied potato-cake into pieces ¾"×2⅓" long and ⅛" thick. Slit the center, leaving the ends intact and pull one end through the slit forming the same shape as maejagwa, thin Korean cookies.
7 Cut the large green onion diagonally and the garland chrysanthemum into 2⅓" lengths.
8 Fry the shelled ginko nuts with salt, peel off the skins and cut them into halves.
9 Fry the beef and sliced round onion in a pot and add the broth. When the broth boils, add the red snapper and arrange all the prepared ingredients around the fish attractively. Garnish with the gingko nuts.

1 Scale off the red snapper and remove the entrails. Slit the fish diagonally.

2 Sprinkle the slits with the salt and black pepper and then the cornstarch powder.

3 Stuff the slits with the seasoned beef, round onion and red pepper mixture.

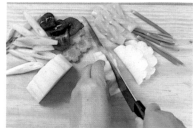

4 Halve the radish and cut it into thin flowerlike shapes.

Octopus Hot Pot
Nakchi Chǒn-gol (낙지 전골)

Ingredients 2 octopuses, ¼ lb. cabbage, 3 oz. spinach, ½ lb. corbicula clam, 1 cake bean curd, 1 large green onion, 1 Korean green pepper, 1 red pepper, 2 tbsp. rice wine, 3 dried brown, oak mushrooms, 1 round onion, 3 cups meat stock, various seasoning

Method **1** Clean and cut the octopuses into 2⅓" long pieces.
2 Parboil the cabbage starting with the stems.

3 Parboil the spinach and mix it with the soy sauce, sesame oil, sugar and salt. Squeeze out the water and wrap it in the scalded cabbage leaf. Cut the rolls into 1¼" lengths.

4 Cut the bean curd into flat pieces ⅓" thick. Cut the green onion into 2" diagonal strips.

5 Soak the clam in salt water overnight and let it stand to remove the sediment.

6 Season the octopus pieces with the red pepper paste, red pepper powder and seasoning. Arrange the prepared ingredients attractively in a casserole.

7 Add the boiling broth to the #6 ingredients, season with salt and bring to a quick boil for the best taste. Serve at once.

1 Clean and cut the octopuses into 2⅓" long pieces.

2 Place the spinach on the cabbage leaf and roll it up.

3 Cut the rolls into 1¼" lengths.

4 Cut the bean curd into ¼" thick pieces and the green onion into 2" diagonal strips.

5 Arrange the prepared ingredients in a casserole and add the seasoned octopus pieces.

Vegetable Hot Pot
Yach'ae Chŏn-gol (야채 전골)

Ingredients ⅔ lb. beef, ¼ lb. konyak: jellied potato-cake, ½ zucchini, ⅓ carrot, 10 pine mushrooms, 1 round onion, 1 large green onion, 3 cabbage leaves, ¼ lb. bean sprouts, 2 tbsp. chopped green onion, 2 tbsp. garlic, ½ tsp. sesame oil, 3 tbsp. soy sauce, 1 tbsp. salt, 1 tbsp. red pepper powder, black pepper, MSG, 5 cups water, ½ bundle garland chrysanthemum

Method **1** Slice the beef into thin strips and season it with the soy sauce, green onion, garlic, sugar, sesame oil and MSG.

2 Cut the jellied potato-cake into ¾″ × 2⅓″ pieces. Slit the center leaving the ends intact and pull one end of each piece through the slit.

3 Slice the zucchini and carrot into half-circles.

4 Peel and slice the pine mushrooms. Cut the round onion and cabbage into thick strips.

5 Cut the large green onion diagonally.

6 Arrange the prepared ingredients attractively in a cooking dish. Place the bean sprouts in the center and top them with the pine mushroom slices. Add the seasoned broth and boil briefly at the table.

3 Peel and slice the pine mushrooms.

4 Slice the squash and carrot into half-circles.

1 Cut the beef into thin strips and season.

2 Shape the jellied potato-cake pieces into the same form as maejagwa.

5 Cut the vegetables into thick strips.

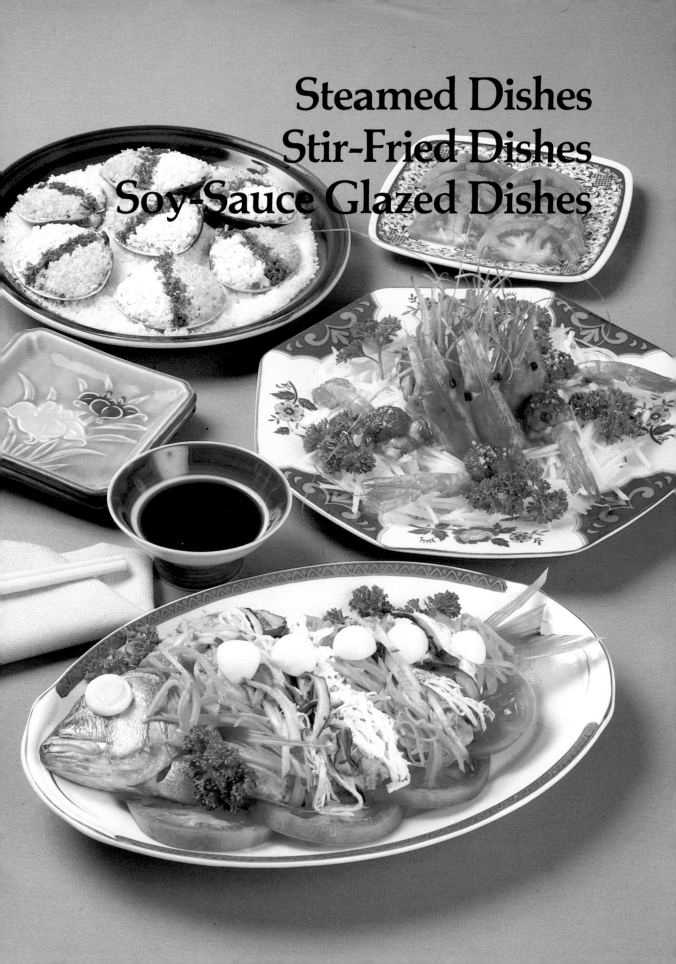

Steamed Dishes
Stir-Fried Dishes
Soy-Sauce Glazed Dishes

Steamed Red Snapper
Tomitchim (도미찜)

Ingredients 1 red snapper, 1 tsp. salt, black pepper, 2 oz. beef, ½ cake bean curd, green onion, garlic, sesame oil, ½ tsp. salt, ½ tsp. sesame salt, 1 tsp. soy sauce, ½ cucumber, ½ carrot, 3 dried brown, oak mushrooms, 2 eggs, 10 quail eggs, ½ tomato, ½ bundle parsley, pine nuts, lemon

Method 1 Clean and scale the red snapper. Fillet the fish keeping the skeleton and head intact. Slice the fish fillets into bite-sized pieces and sprinkle them with the salt and black pepper.

2 Chop the beef finely. Squeeze out the water from the bean curd. Mix the beef and bean curd with the soy sauce, green onion, garlic, sesame oil and sesame salt.

3 Cut the cucumber into thin strips and sprinkle it with salt. Squeeze out the water and fry lightly.

4 Soak the dried mushrooms and cut them into thin strips. Sprinkle them with the soy sauce and sugar and fry.

5 Cut the carrot into thin strips and sprinkle it with salt and fry. Fry the egg white and egg yolk separately into sheets and cut them into thin strips.

6 Dip the red snapper slices into flour. Wrap the beef and pine nut in the fish slice and roll. Then dip the rolls into beaten egg and fry until brown.

7 Place the fried fish rolls on the fish skeleton. Cover with the vegetables alternating colors. Steam the stuffed red snapper on a steamer rack until tender for 10-15 minutes.

8 Boil and peel the quail eggs and cut them in half. Garnish with the quail egg, tomato and parsley.

Hint 1 When serving the whole red snapper, place the head of the red snapper at the left of the plate.

2 If the plate has too much liquid in it after steaming the fish, remove the fish to a dry plate.

1 Clean and scale the red snapper. Fillet the fish.

2 Chop the beef finely. Squeeze out the water from the bean curd and season.

3 Cut the cucumber, dried mushrooms and carrot into thin strips and fry them separately.

4 Cut the two fillets into bite-sized pieces. Place the #2 mixture and pine nuts on the fish slice and roll.

5 Dip the rolls into flour and egg and fry until brown.

Ingredients   3 cups ark shell clams, 4 tbsp. soy sauce, ½ tbsp. sugar, 1 tbsp. red pepper powder, 2 tbsp. chopped garlic, 4 tbsp. chopped green onion, 2 tbsp. sesame salt, 1 tbsp. sesame oil, red pepper thread, pine nuts, lettuce

Method   **1** Clean the ark shell clams by rubbing them with salt and soak them in salt water so that the clams will spit out the watery sediment; drain.

2 Mix the soy sauce, chopped green onion, garlic, red pepper thread, red pepper powder, sesame salt, black pepper and sesame oil to make the seasoning sauce.

3 Scald the ark shells or steam them in a steamer. Remove one side of the shell and the organs from the clam meat. Re-place the meat in the shells, sprinkle with the seasoning sauce and top them with the pine nut.

1 Clean the ark shells and scald them in boiling water.

3 Remove the organ from the ark shell neatly.

2 Remove one side of the shell, leaving the other side to which the flesh is attached.

4 Sprinkle the seasoning sauce on the clam meat.

6 Place the fried rolls on the skeleton.

7 Top the skeleton with the prepared vegetables alternating colors.

8 Steam on a rack in the steamer for 10-15 minutes.

Steamed Abalones
Chonboktchim (전복찜)

Ingredients 6 abalones, 3 walnuts, 6 gingko nuts, 3 tbsp. soy sauce, 1½ tbsp. sugar, 1 tbsp. rice wine, 3 cloves garlic, 1 knob ginger, black pepper, sesame oil, ½ cup water, 2 cups green sweet peas, radish, parsley

Method **1** Clean the abalones and scald in boiling salted water.

2 Remove the shells and entrails from the abalones. Score the insides at ¼" intervals crosswise and lengthwise.

3 Soak the walnuts in hot water and peel off the inner skin using a toothpick.

4 Fry the shelled ginko nuts with salt until the color becomes green; rub off the skins.

5 Boil the seasoning sauce in a pan, add the abalones and simmer.

6 On a skewer, string the gingko nut, abalone and walnut alternately. Place the skewered food on the shell of the abalone.

7 Boil the green peas in salted water and stir-fry lightly. Spread them on a plate and arrange the abalone in the shells on top. Garnish with the red radish and parsley.

3 Score the insides of the abalones.

4 Peel the inner skin off the walnuts using a toothpick.

1 Clean the abalones and scald them in boiling water.

2 Remove the shells and entrails from the abalones and clean.

5 Add the abalones to the boiling seasoning sauce and simmer.

92

Steamed Stuffed Clams
Taehaptchim (대합찜)

Ingredients   **A.** 4 large clams, 2 oz. beef, ½ cake bean curd, 1 egg, ¼ tsp. salt, 1 tsp. sesame salt, 1 tsp. sesame oil, green onion, garlic, black pepper
B. 1 egg, ½ bundle parsley, 2 cups coarse salt

Method   **1** Soak the large clams in water overnight, so that they spit out the sand and watery sediment.
2 Clean the clams and scald them in boiling water. Remove the clam meat from the shell and chop it finely. Clean the shells and set aside.
3 Fry the chopped beef lightly in a greased pan and chop it finely again. Fry the beaten egg yolk and white separately into thin sheets.
4 Squeeze out the excess water from the bean curd and mash.
5 Mix the chopped clam meat, beef, beaten egg and bean curd with the **A** seasonings. Fill the trimmed shells with the mixture and garnish them with fine strips of the cooked egg white and yolk and parsley.
6 Place the stuffed shells on a steamer rack in the steamer and steam for 10 minutes. Arrange the steamed stuffed clams on coarse salt on a plate.

1 Scald the large clams in boiling water.

3 Chop the beef and the clam meat.

5 Season the chopped beef, clam meat and mashed bean curd.

2 Chop the beef finely and fry.

4 Fry the beaten egg yolk and white separately.

6 Fill the clam shells with the #5 mixture and garnish.

Steamed Stuffed Crabs
Ketchim (게찜)

Ingredients 3 red crabs, ¼ lb. beef, 1 cake bean curd, 2 eggs, 1 large green onion, 4 cloves garlic, ½ tsp. sesame oil, 1 tsp salt, black pepper, 3 stone mushrooms, red pepper thread, lettuce, parsley

Method **1** Scrub the crabs with salt and clean. Leaving the large legs intact, remove the bottom shells and small legs from the crabs. Remove the crab meat from the shells and place it in a bowl.

2 Mince the beef finely; squeeze out the water from the bean curd.

3 Combine the crab meat, minced beef, bean curd, green onion, garlic, egg, sesame oil, salt and black pepper.

4 Soak the stone mushrooms in water and cut them into thin strips. Fry the beaten egg yolk and white into sheets separately and cut them into thin strips.

5 Grease the insides of the crab shells and fill with the #3 mixture. Top them with the stone mushroom, egg strips and red pepper threads and steam with the large legs in a steamer. Garnish with the parsley on lettuce on a plate.

3 Season the crab meat, beef and bean curd.

1 Remove the bottom shells and legs from the crabs.

4 Fill the crab shells with the #3 mixture.

2 Remove the crab meat from the shells.

5 Steam the stuffed crabs and legs in a steamer.

Steamed Conches
Soratchim 〔소라찜〕

Ingredients 6 Top-shell, 1 egg, ½ bundle parsley, 1 red pepper, sesame oil, salt, 3 boiled ears of corn, 2 stone mushrooms

Method 1 Clean and steam the Top-shell in a steamer.

2 Fry the beaten egg yolk and white separately into sheets and cut them into thin strips.

3 Remove the seeds from the red pepper and cut it into short, thin strips. Chop the parsley finely.

4 Soak the stone mushrooms in water and cut them into thin strips.

5 Take the meat out of the boiled Top-shell and remove the entrails. Slice thinly and mix with the salt and sesame oil.

6 Fill the shells with the seasoned Top-shell meat and garnish with the egg and vegetable strips.

7 Place the fried boiled corn on a plate and place the stuffed conches on the corn. Garnish with the parsley.

Hint When you steam the food, add the food to the steamer after the water boils. The inside of the steamer and the food get wet if you add the food to the steamer when the temperature is too low.

3 Take the Top-shell meat out of the shells and slice thinly; season it with the salt and sesame oil.

4 Fill the Top-shell with the seasoned meat and garnish.

1 Clean and steam the Top-shell in a steamer.

2 Chop the parsley finely. Cut the egg sheets and vegetables into thin strips.

Steamed Stuffed Eggplant
Kajitchim (가지찜)

Ingredients   3 eggplants, salt, 2 oz. beef, ½ cake bean curd, 1 round onion, ½ green onion, 1 clove garlic, 1 tbsp. red pepper paste, 1 tbsp. soy sauce, 1 tbsp. sesame salt, black pepper, MSG, 1 tbsp. sesame oil, ½ cup meat stock

Method   1 Halve small sleek eggplant. Slit each piece twice through the middle, with the two cuts at right angles leaving the ends intact. Soak them in salt water and then squeeze out the water.

2 Mince the beef finely and squeeze out the excess water from the bean curd. Mix the seasoning with the beef and bean curd. Stuff the slits with the mixture.

3 Place the stuffed eggplants on a layer of sliced round onions in a pot. Add the meat stock and simmer; or steam in a steamer.

1 Cut the scalded cabbage leaves and vegetables into thin strips.

2 Season the vegetables well with the salt, black pepper and sesame oil.

1 Halve the eggplants, and slit each piece at right angles.

2 Stuff the slits with the seasoned mashed bean curd and minced beef.

3 Place the stuffed eggplants on a layer of the sliced round onion in a pot and simmer.

Steamed Cabbage and Vegetables
Yangbaech'u Yach'aetchim (양배추 야채찜)

3 Sprinkle the **#2** vegetables with some flour and mix them into the thick dough.

4 Shape the dough into a square patty and steam in a steamer.

5 Scald the green beans in salt water. Fry in butter and wrap them firmly in the sheet of laver.

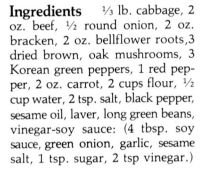

Ingredients   ⅓ lb. cabbage, 2 oz. beef, ½ round onion, 2 oz. bracken, 2 oz. bellflower roots, 3 dried brown, oak mushrooms, 3 Korean green peppers, 1 red pepper, 2 oz. carrot, 2 cups flour, ½ cup water, 2 tsp. salt, black pepper, sesame oil, laver, long green beans, vinegar-soy sauce: (4 tbsp. soy sauce, green onion, garlic, sesame salt, 1 tsp. sugar, 2 tsp vinegar.)

Method   **1** Remove the thick veins from the cabbage. Scald the cabbage and cut it into thin strips. **2** Slice the beef into thin strips and season. Soak the dried mushrooms in water and remove the stems. Slice them into thin strips. **3** Parboil the bracken and bellflower roots and cut them into 2″ lengths. Cut the carrot into thin strips and scald.
4 Halve the green peppers and red pepper and remove the seeds. Cut them into thick strips.
5 Season the vegetable strips with the salt, black pepper, MSG and sesame oil and sprinkle them with the flour.
6 Knead the flour with water to make a thick dough. Then mix the dough with the **#7** seasoned vegetables.
7 Shape the **#8** mixture into a square patty and steam it in a damp cloth in the steamer.
8 Cut the cooled steamed patty into bite-sized pieces. Scald the green beans and stir-fry lightly. Wrap them in the sheet of laver and cut diagonally. Arrange the steamed vegetable pieces and green bean bundles on a plate. Serve with vinegar-soy sauce.

Steamed Stuffed Fish
Ŏsŏn (어선)

Ingredients   1 pollack, ½ bundle watercress, ¼ lb. carrot, 6 dried brown, oak mushrooms, 2 eggs, 1 tbsp. salt, 5 tbsp. cornstarch powder, 4 cabbage leaves, 1 tsp. sesame oil, 1 tomato, parsley, 3 tbsp. soy sauce, 1 tsp. vinegar, 1 tsp. pine nut

Method   **1** Slice the pollack thinly and sprinkle with the salt and black pepper.
2 Trim and clean the watercress. Stir-fry the stems mixing them with the salt and sesame oil.
3 Soak the dried mushrooms in water, squeeze out the water. Cut them into thin strips and season them with the soy sauce, sugar, and sesame oil and fry.
4 Cut the carrot into thin strips and fry sprinkling with salt.
5 Fry the beaten egg yolk and white separately into sheets and cut them into thin strips.
6 Dip the pollack slices into the cornstarch powder. Place the watercress, carrot, dried mushroom and egg strips on each fish slice and wrap the fish around them firmly.
7 Place the #6 rolls on a damp cloth in a steamer and steam. Cool the steamed rolls and cut them into 1⅔" lengths.
8 Mix the soy sauce, vinegar and chopped pine nuts to make the vinegar-soy sauce.
9 Place a layer of shredded cabbage on a plate and arrange the sliced fish rolls attractively. Garnish with the tomato and parsley. Serve with vinegar-soy sauce for dipping.

1 Slice the pollack thinly and sprinkle with the salt and black pepper.

2 Fry the watercress, carrot and dried mushrooms separately.

3 Place the vegetable and egg strips on the pollack slice dipped into the starch powder, and wrap them firmly.

Stuffed Zucchini
Hobaksŏn (호박선)

Ingredients 2 young zucchini, ¼ lb. beef, 1 tsp. sesame salt, 2 tsp. soy sauce, ½ tsp. salt, 1 tsp. sesame oil, black pepper, 2 tsp. chopped garlic 1 tbsp. chopped green onion, 3 dried brown, oak mushrooms, 1 egg, 1 round onion, 1 cup meat stock, 1 stone mushroom, pine nuts, salt, red pepper thread

Method **1** Choose tender, straight zucchini and cut them into 2″ lengths. Put X slits on the zucchini chunks and sprinkle them with salt.

4 Steam the rolls on a damp cloth in a steamer.

2 Soak the dried mushrooms in water to soften and remove the stems. Cut them into thin strips.
3 Combine the minced beef, dried mushroom strips, sesame salt, soy sauce, salt, sesame oil, black pepper, chopped green onion and garlic.
4 Halve the round onion and cut it into thin strips.
5 Fry the beaten egg yolk and white separately into thin sheets and cut them into thin strips.
6 Stuff the squash with the egg strips and red pepper thread.
7 Place the stuffed squash chunks on a layer of sliced round onion in a pot.
8 Add 1 cup of meat broth seasoned with the soy sauce, salt and black pepper and bring to a boil.

Hint In order not to cut the zucchini too far, place the zucchini pieces between two wooden chopsticks. They will stop the knife before it cuts all the way through the zucchini.

1 Put X slits in the zucchini chunks placed between two chopsticks.

2 Sprinkle the zucchini chunks with salt.

3 Stuff the slits with the seasoned beef.

4 Place the stuffed zucchini chunks on a layer of sliced round onion in a pot.

Fried Octopus
Nakchibokkŭm (낙지볶음)

2 Rub the octopus pieces with salt and rinse clean.

4 When the garlic is cooked, add the round onion, carrot and the seasoned red pepper paste.

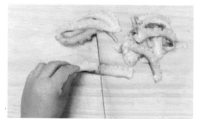

1 Clean and cut the octopuses into 2⅓" lengths.

3 Cut the carrot, round onions and green peppers into rectangular pieces.

5 Fry the octopus pieces with the #4 mixture and sprinkle the sesame oil and sesame seed last of all.

Ingredients   3 octopuses, 1 green onion, 2 round onions, ½ carrot, black pepper, 1 tbsp. sugar, 3 tbsp. red pepper paste, 2 tbsp. red pepper powder, 2 tbsp. soy sauce, MSG, ginger juice, green onion, garlic, sesame oil, sesame seed, Korean green peppers

Method   **1** Rub the octopuses with salt and rinse clean. Cut them into 2⅓" lengths.

2 Remove the seeds from the green peppers. Cut them and the carrot into rectangles. Halve the round onions and slice them the same size as the carrot pieces.

3 Slice the garlic; cut the green onion diagonally.

4 Fry the garlic, carrot and round onion lightly in an oiled pan; add the red pepper paste, red pepper powder, soy sauce, sugar, green onion, green pepper and octopus pieces and continue to fry. When done, sprinkle on the sesame oil and sesame seed and mix well.

Hint   You may rub the octopuses with salt to clean them after cutting them into pieces.

100

Fried Young Squash
Aehobakpokkŭm (애호박볶음)

Ingredients 1 young squash (zucchini), 2 oz. beef, 1 large green onion, 4 cloves garlic, 2 tsp. sesame salt, 2 tsp. sesame oil, 2 tbsp. soused salted shrimp juice, soy sauce, red pepper thread, salt

Method **1** Halve the young squash and cut it into half-circle pieces. Sprinkle the squash pieces with salt and let them stand.
2 Slice the beef and season it with the green onion, garlic, sesame salt, sesame oil and soy sauce.
3 Squeeze the water out from the salted squash and stir-fry lightly; place it on a plate.
4 Fry the beef and mix it with the squash pieces, shredded red pepper thread and season it with the salted shrimp juice.

Hint **1** Fry the young squash separately and add it to the fried beef later for a fresher taste.
2 Fry the squash briefly because it loses its taste if cooked too long.

1 Cut the young squash into half-circle pieces, sprinkle it with salt and let it stand.

3 Squeeze the water out from the squash and fry lightly.

4 After frying the beef, add the squash pieces and fry lightly.

2 Slice the beef and season.

5 Season with the soused salted shrimp juice and red pepper thread.

Stir-Fried Anchovies with Peppers
Putkoch'u Myŏlch'ibokkŭm (풋고추 멸치볶음)

Ingredients ⅓ lb. Korean-style long green peppers, ¼ lb. dried anchovies, 3 tbsp. soy sauce, 2 cloves garlic, 1½ tbsp. sugar, 1 tsp. sesame oil, 2 tbsp. salad oil, sesame seed, red pepper thread

Method 1 Wash the small green peppers and drain. Remove the stems.
2 Trim the small dried anchovies carefully.
3 Slice the garlic.
4 Stir-fry the anchovies and garlic lightly in an oiled pan. Add the soy sauce and sugar and then the green peppers and fry a bit more.
5 When the ingredients are almost cooked, add the sesame oil and red pepper thread and mix well.

Hint 1 Choose small-sized dried anchovies. Fry the green peppers quickly in order to keep the green color.
2 Choose the long Korean peppers (not hot).

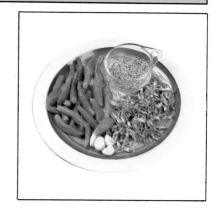

1 Fry the dried anchovies and garlic in a greased pan.

2 Add the seasoning and the green peppers to #1 and fry.

3 When the ingredients are almost done, add the sesame oil, sesame seed and red pepper thread and fry.

Sea Mussel in Soy Sauce
Honghapch'o (홍합초)

Ingredients   A. ¼ lb. dried sea mussels, 2 oz. beef
B. 5 tbsp. soy sauce, 3 tbsp. sugar, 5 cloves garlic, ½ oz. ginger, 1 cup water
C. sesame seed

Method   1 Slice the garlic and ginger in thin pieces.
2 Soak the dried sea mussels in water to soften.
3 Simmer the sliced beef and sea mussel seasoned with the garlic, ginger and the **B** ingredients until glazed.
4 Place the **#3** simmered ingredients in a bowl and sprinkle with sesame seed.

1 Slice the garlic and ginger in thin pieces.

2 Slice the beef.

3 Add the **#1**, **#2** ingredients to the sea mussels and simmer.

Abalones in Soy Sauce
Chŏnbokch'o (전복초)

Ingredients 6 abalones, ⅓ cup sweet soy sauce, 2 cabbage leaves, powdered pine nuts, parsley

Method **1** Wash the abalones and scald them in salt water. Remove the shells, entrails and lips of the abalones.

2 Score the trimmed abalones crosswise and lengthwise.

3 Simmer the scored abalones with sweet soy sauce until glazed.

4 Place the simmered abalones in the cleaned shells and sprinkle them with the powdered pine nuts.

5 Arrange the #4 abalones on shredded cabbage on a plate and garnish with the parsley.

Hint **1** Scald the abalone to make it tender and then remove the meat from the shell.

2 You may place the abalone meat directly on a plate instead of the shells.

3 Score the back side of the abalone meat.

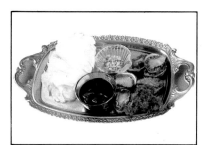

1 Wash the abalones and scald in hot water.

4 Simmer the abalones in the sweet soy sauce.

2 Remove the shells and organs from the abalones.

5 Place the abalone meat in the shells and sprinkle with powdered pine nuts.

Soy-Sauce Glazed Cutlass-Fish
Kalch'ijorim (갈치조림)

Ingredients 1 cutlass-fish, salt, black pepper, ½ white Korean radish, 3 cloves garlic, 1 large green onion, 1 tbsp. red pepper powder, 4 tbsp. soy sauce, 2 tbsp. sugar, 1 knob ginger, ½ cup cornstarch powder, oil

Method **1** Scrape the skin of the cutlass-fish with the knife and remove the entrails. Wash it and cut it into pieces 2¾″ long. Slit each piece at ¼″ intervals and sprinkle with the salt and black pepper.

2 Cut the radish into pieces 1¼″ long and cut X slit on each piece. Scald in boiling water and drain.

3 Dip the cutlass-fish pieces into the cornstarch powder and deep-fry them in oil.

4 Boil the **#2** radish pieces with the soy sauce, red pepper powder, green onion, garlic, sugar, ginger and water in a pot. When it boils, add the **#3** cutlass-fish pieces and sprinkle with the red pepper powder.

1 Trim and cut the cutlass-fish into pieces 2¾″ long and score them at ¼″ intervals.

2 Dip the cutlass-fish into the cornstarch powder and deep-fry in oil.

3 Put X slits on the radish pieces.

4 Simmer the radish in the seasoning sauce.

5 Add the deep-fried cutlass-fish to **#4** and simmer.

Soy-Sauce Glazed Mackerel Pike Meatballs
Kkongch'iwanjajorim (꽁치완자조림)

Ingredients 2 mackerel pikes, ½ round onion, ½ carrot, 2 cloves garlic, 1 knob ginger, ½ cucumber, ¼ carrot, 3 tbsp. soy sauce, 2 tbsp. red pepper powder, 1 tsp. sugar, ½ tbsp. salt, black pepper, ⅓ cup bread flour, flour, 1 egg, frying oil, 10 skewers

Method **1** Remove the thick bones and entrails from the mackerel. Rinse, dry and chop finely.
2 Chop the carrot and round onion finely and sprinkle them with salt. Squeeze out the water.
3 Mix the chopped mackerel pike meat, round onion and carrot with the green onion, garlic, ginger, salt, black pepper and bread flour. Knead and shape the mixture into meatballs ¾" in diameter. Dip the meatballs into flour and then into beaten egg and deep-fry them in oil.
4 Boil ½ cup of water with the soy sauce, garlic, ginger, red pepper powder and sugar. Add the meatballs and simmer.
5 String the cucumber and meatballs on skewers and place them on a paper doily on a plate. Garnish with the flower-shaped carrot.

2 Chop the round onion and carrot finely and sprinkle them with salt.

4 Shape the **#3** mixture into meatballs, dip them in flour and then into beaten egg and deep-fry in oil.

1 Remove the mackerel from the bones and rinse.

3 Mix **#1** and **#2** with the bread flour, soy sauce, salt, sugar, green onion and garlic.

5 Add the deep-fried meatballs to the boiling seasoning sauce and simmer.

Soy-Sauce Glazed Burdock Root
Uŏngjorim (우엉조림)

Ingredients   ½ lb. burdock root, ¼ lb. beef, ¼ lb. konyak: jellied potato-cake, ⅔ cup soy sauce, ⅓ cup sugar, ¼ cup rice wine, 1½ cup water, pine nut powder

Method   **1** Peel and scald the burdock root and cut it into thick strips.
2 Cut the beef into ¼" thick strips.
3 Cut the jellied potato-cake into ¾"×2⅓" long and ⅛" thick pieces. Score the center leaving the ends intact and pull one end of each piece through the slits. (Shape each piece into the same form as maejagwa.)
4 Place the beef, burdock root and jellied potato-cake pieces with the seasoning in a pot, cover and simmer. When the liquid is almost evaporated, remove the lid and simmer on high heat until glazed.
5 Place the food in a bowl and sprinkle it with the powdered pine nuts.

1 Peel and cut the burdock root into chunks and then scald it in boiling water.

2 Cut the beef and burdock root into thick strips.

3 Place the beef, burdock root and jellied potato-cake pieces in a pot and simmer until glazed.

Soy-Sauce Glazed Lotus Root
Yŏn-gŭnjorim (연근조림)

Ingredients ⅔ lb. lotus root, ¼ lb. beef, ½ round onion, ½ cup soy sauce, 4 tbsp. black sugar, 4 tbsp. rice wine, 1½ oz. dark corn syrup, 2 tbsp. oil, vinegar, sesame salt, MSG, 2 cups water, radish, parsley

Method **1** Peel the lotus root and slice it into pieces ¼" thick.
2 Sprinkle the sliced lotus root in vinegar, drop in boiling water, remove and trim the edges into flowerlike shapes.
3 Slice the beef. Cut the round onion into pieces ⅓" square.
4 Simmer the sliced lotus root with the seasoning on low heat in an oiled pan.
5 When the **#5** seasoning is almost evaporated, add the beef and round onion and simmer on high heat until glazed.
6 Garnish with the red radish and parsley.

Hint In order to keep the sliced lotus root white, you may add salt, vinegar and sugar to it or put it in vinegar-water.

1 Sprinkle the lotus root with vinegar and drop into boiling water.

3 Simmer the lotus root with the seasoning.

2 Trim the edges of the sliced lotus root into flowerlike shapes.

Broiled Foods
Deep-Fried Foods
Skewered Foods
Pan-Fried Foods

Broiled Spanish Mackerel
Samch'i Sogŭmgui (삼치 소금구이)

Ingredients   1 Spanish mackerel, 3 tbsp. salt, ¼ radish, cucumber, lemon, parsley

Method   **1** Scale and clean the Spanish mackerel. Remove the entrails. Cut the fish into four pieces and put X slits on both sides.

2 Sprinkle the pieces with the salt and let them stand.

3 Broil the salted fish on a heated oiled grill. When using an oven-broiler, place the fish in a heated pan and broil.

4 Place the broiled fish pieces on a layer of shredded white radish on a plate and garnish with the parsley, lemon and cucumber.

Hint   After scoring the fish pieces, marinate them in the seasoning sauce. Then broil them on a grill, basting the fish with the seasoning sauce.

1 Remove the entrails from the Spanish mackerel. Clean and cut it into pieces.

3 Sprinkle the fish pieces with the salt and let them stand.

2 Put X slits on both sides of the pieces.

4 Broil on a heated oiled grill.

110

Seasoned Broiled Eel
Changŏ Yangnyŏmgui (장어 양념구이)

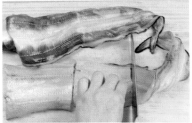

1 Clean the eels and cut them into pieces 4″.

3 Broil the eel pieces on a heated oiled grill.

Ingredients **A** 2 eels

B 1 tsp. ginger juice, 1½ tbsp. sugar, 1 tbsp. rice wine, 5 tbsp. soy sauce, 3 tbsp. chopped green onion, 1 tbsp. chopped garlic, sesame salt, black pepper, sesame oil, 3 tbsp. water

C 1 cucumber, 1 red pepper

Method **1** Choose fresh, live eels. Remove the heads and the entrails. Halve and slice the eels.

2 Boil the **B** ingredients slightly to make a thick seasoning sauce.

3 Pound the sliced eels with the tip of the knife and cut them into pieces. Broil the pieces on a heated grill.

4 Baste the eels with the seasoning sauce and broil again.

5 Place the broiled eels in a dish and garnish with the cucumber and red pepper.

2 Boil the **B** ingredients to make the thick seasoning sauce.

4 Baste the eels with the seasoning sauce and broil again.

Broiled Squid
Ojingŏgui (오징어구이)

Ingredients   2 squid, 2 tbsp. soy sauce, 2 green onions, 2 tbsp. red pepper paste, ½ tbsp. sugar, 1 tbsp. chopped garlic, ½ tbsp. sesame salt, 2 red peppers, 2 long Korean green peppers, sesame oil, red pepper thread, black pepper, MSG

Method   **1** Halve the fresh squid lengthwise and clean.
2 Flatten the squid and skin it by rubbing it with the salt.
3 Dry and score the inside of the squid crosswise and lengthwise at 1″ intervals. Cut it into pieces 1⅔″ × 2″
4 Scald the squid pieces in boiling water and drain.
5 Make the seasoning sauce with the red pepper paste and soy sauce.
6 Baste the squid pieces with the seasoning sauce and broil the squid on medium heat on a grill.
7 Garnish with the red pepper.
Hint   You can skin the body of the squid by rubbing it with a cloth dipped into salt.

2 Halve the squid and cut diagonal slits.

4 Scald the squid pieces in boiling water.

1 Skin the body of the squid.

3 Cut the scored squid into bite-sized pieces.

5 Baste with the seasoning sauce and broil on a grill.

Seasoned Broiled Corvina
Chogi Yangnyomgui (조기 양념구이)

Ingredients 1 corvina, 2 tbsp. soy sauce, 1 tbsp. vinegar, 1 tbsp. sesame salt, 1 tbsp. chopped green onion, ½ tbsp. garlic, ginger juice, 2 tsp. red pepper powder, 2 tsp. sesame oil, 1 tsp. sugar, black pepper, ½ tomato, lettuce, ¼ cucumber

Method 1 Select fresh yellow corvina. Clean the corvina removing the entrails and the scales. Wash well and pat dry.

2 Put deep slits on both sides of the fish at ¾" intervals.

3 Mix the soy sauce with the seasoning to make the seasoning sauce.

4 Baste the corvina with the seasoning sauce and broil it on medium heat on a heated oiled grill until golden-brown.

5 Serve the broiled corvina on a plate with the lettuce leaves, tomato and cucumber.

2 Mix the seasoning to make the seasoning sauce.

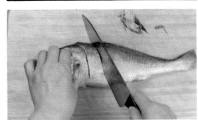

1 Clean the fish and score deeply on both sides of the fish at ¾" intervals.

3 Baste the fish with the seasoning sauce and broil on an oiled grill.

113

Broiled Trout
Songŏgui (송어구이)

Ingredients 1 trout, 4 tbsp. salt, ½ lemon, soy sauce, rice wine, sugar, lettuce

Method 1 Clean the trout removing the fin and entrails. Divide the fish into half and remove the flesh from the bones.
2 Cut the trout into appropriately sized pieces and put slits through the skin. Sprinkle the fish pieces with the salt and let them stand.
3 When well-salted, broil the fish on a heated oiled grill.
4 Place the broiled fish on lettuce leaves on a plate and garnish with the lemon slices.

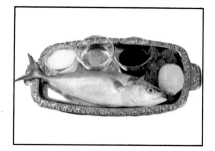

1 Cut through the skin of the fish pieces.

2 Sprinkle the fish pieces with the salt and let them stand.

3 Broil on a heated oiled grill.

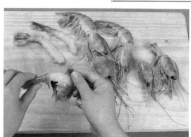

1 Remove the head and the shell from the prawn leaving the tail area including the second joint intact.

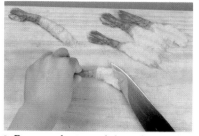

2 Remove the innards by splitting the back of the prawn and sprinkle with the salt.

3 Shape the beef and bean curd mixture into the meatballs and place one meatball on each prawn.

114

Broiled Prawns
Taehagui (대하구이)

Ingredients   5 prawns, 1 oz. beef, ¼ cake bean curd, salt, black pepper, garlic, sesame oil, sweet soy sauce, radish, parsley, pine nut powder

Method   **1** Remove the head and the shell from the prawns leaving the tail area including the second joint intact. Remove the innards by splitting the back of the prawn and sprinkle with salt.

2 Mince the beef finely. Squeeze out the water from the bean curd and mash.

3 Mix the minced beef and mashed bean curd with the seasoning. Shape the mixture by tablespoonfuls into the oval meatballs. Place each meatball on a prawn.

4 Broil the prawns in a fry pan or an oven-broiler for 10 minutes. Then baste them with sweet soy sauce and broil again.

5 Place the broiled prawns on a layer of shredded white radish on a plate. Sprinkle with the powdered pine nuts and garnish with the parsley.

4 Broil the prawns and the heads for 10 minutes in an oven-broiler.

5 Baste them with sweet soy sauce and broil again.

115

Broiled Todok
Tŏdŏkkui (더덕구이)

Ingredients   15 todoks (a white root), 2 tbsp. red pepper paste, ½ tbsp. red pepper powder, 2 tbsp. soy sauce, 1 tbsp. chopped garlic, 2 tbsp. chopped green onion, 1 tbsp. sugar, 1 tbsp. sesame salt, 2 tbsp. sesame oil, salt

Method   **1** After soaking and peeling the todok, remove the bitterness by soaking the todok in salt water; then pat them dry. Slice the todok thinly and pound it flat with a mallet.

2 Mix the red pepper paste with the soy sauce, green onion, garlic, sesame salt and sesame oil. Simmer the mixture until thickened.

3 Broil the todok on a grill and baste it with the seasoned red pepper paste.

1 Remove the bitterness by soaking the todok in salt water.

3 Pound the thinly sliced todok flat with the mallet.

2 Pat the todok dry with a dry cloth.

4 Baste the broiled todok with the seasoned red pepper paste.

Deep-Fried Shrimp
Saeut'wigim (새우튀김)

Ingredients **A** 6 shrimp, 2 eggs, ½ cup flour, salt, black pepper
B ½ cup white sesame seed, ½ cup black sesame seed, ½ cup peanut powder
C ginger juice, 2 tbsp. soy sauce, 1 tbsp. rice wine, 6 tbsp. kelp broth
D lemon, parsley

Method **1** Prepare fresh, large shrimp by removing the shells from the shrimps leaving the tail area including the second joint intact.
2 Remove the entrails by splitting the back, and cut off the red fibers from the legs. Tenderize the shrimp by pounding them with the back of the knife. Sprinkle the shrimp with the salt and black pepper.

3 Dust the shrimp (except the tail area) evenly with flour.
4 Mix the beaten egg and flour to make a thick paste.
5 Dip the shrimp into the thick paste and then into the black sesame seed, white sesame seed and peanut powder. Deep-fry them in oil at 340°F.
6 Boil the **C** seasonings and remove the froth from the top.
7 Stand the shrimps on end on a plate and garnish with the parsley and lemon. Serve with the #6 seasoning sauce.

Hint Cut ⅛" from the tail of the shrimp, otherwise the oil may splash and burn you when adding the shrimp to the boiling oil.

1 Trim and score the shrimp at ⅓" intervals.

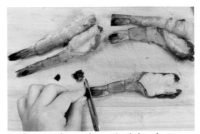
2 Cut ½ from the tail of the shrimp.

3 Dust the shrimp (except the tail area) with flour.

4 Mix the beaten egg and flour to make a thick paste.

5 Dip the shrimp into the thick paste and then into the black sesame seed and peanut powder and deep-fry.

Deep-Fried Vegetables
Yach'aet'wigim （야채튀김）

Ingredients   1 potato, ½ carrot, 5 sesame leaves, 4 stems garland chrysanthemum, 1 round onion, 1 burdock root, 3 green peppers, 1 cup flour, 1 egg yolk, ⅔ cup ice water, frying oil

Method   **1** Peel the potato and cut it into circles ¼" thick. Wash it in salt water.

2 Trim the sesame leaves and garland chrysanthemum. Slice the round onion into ¼" thick disks and insert a toothpick through the layers.

3 Cut the carrot into thin strips. Peel and cut the burdock root into pieces. Scald the burdock pieces and cut them into thin strips. Soak them in cold water to remove any discoloration.

4 Score the green peppers slightly.

5 Mix the egg yolk and flour with ⅔ cup ice water to make a thick paste.

6 Dip the prepared vegetables into the thick paste and deep-fry them briefly in oil at 360°F.

1 Cut the potato into ¼" thick disks and soak it in salt water.

2 Peel the burdock root and soak it in cold water. Cut the burdock root and carrot into thin strips.

3 Cut the round onion into ¼" thick disks and insert a toothpick through the layers.

4 Score the clean green peppers.

5 Mix the ice water, egg yolk and flour to make a thick paste.

6 Dip the prepared vegetables into the thick paste and deep-fry them.

Deep-Fried Kelp
Tashimat'wigim (다시마튀김)

1 Wrap the kelp in a damp cloth.

3 Remove the tops from the pine nuts.

5 Cut both edges into a deep-V like a ribbon.

2 Cut the kelp into ⅓″ × 4″ pieces.

4 Slip the pine nut into the knot.

6 Deep-fry the kelp until crisp in oil at 340°F and sprinkle with sugar.

Ingredients   1 piece kelp, ¼ cup pine nuts, sugar, oil

Method   **1** Wrap the kelp in a damp cloth.
2 When the kelp gets moist, cut it into ⅓″ × 4″ pieces.
3 Remove the tops from the pine nuts.
4 Tie the kelp like a ribbon and place the pine nut in the center.
5 Cut both edges neatly with a scissors.

6 Heat the oil to 340°F and deep-fry the ribbon-shaped kelp until crisp. Drain and sprinkle with the sugar.
7 Arrange the deep-fried kelp attractively on paper in a basket.
Hint   Deep-fry the kelp on medium heat in oil until crisp. This is a tasty dried side dish with wine.

119

Oysters Fried in Egg Batter
Kuljŏn (굴전)

1 Clean the oysters in salt water and drain.

3 Dip the **#2** oysters into flour.

2 Sprinkle the clean oysters with the ginger juice and black pepper and mix well.

4 Dip the **#3** oysters into beaten egg and fry in an oiled pan.

Ingredients ⅔ lb. oysters, ½ cup flour, 2 eggs, 10 gingko nuts, ginger juice, salt, black pepper, parsley, MSG

Method **1** Buy fresh, large oysters. Wash them in salt water, remove the shells and drain.
2 Sprinkle the clean oysters with the black pepper and ginger juice.
3 Dip the oysters into flour and then into the beaten egg. Fry them in a hot oiled pan.
4 Stir-fry the shelled gingko nuts with salt and peel off the skin.
5 Arrange the fried oysters in a dish and garnish with the ginko nuts and parsley.

120

Fried Stuffed Pepper
P'utkoch'ujŏn (풋고추전)

Ingredients 10 small, long Korean green peppers, 2 red peppers, 2 green bell peppers, ⅓ lb. beef, ⅓ cake bean curd, ½ tsp. soy sauce, 1 tsp. salt, 1 green onion, 4 cloves garlic, 1 tbsp. sesame salt, ¼ tsp. black pepper, 2 tsp. sesame oil, 2 eggs, flour

Method **1** Halve the small green and red peppers. Cut the bell peppers into ¼" thick rings. Remove the seeds.
2 Soak the #1 peppers in salt water and then pat dry. Dip the insides of the pepper halves lightly into flour.
3 Mix the minced beef and mashed bean curd with the seasoning.
4 Stuff the pepper halves and bell pepper rings with the beef mixture.
5 Dip the stuffed side of the pepper into flour and then into beaten egg and fry in a pan until the meat gets cooked through. Dip both sides of the stuffed bell pepper into flour, then into beaten egg and fry until golden brown.

Hint The green pepper contains good amounts of vitamin A. The hot taste of the pepper quickens the secretion of gastric juice and the circulation of the blood.

1 Halve the peppers, slice the bell peppers and remove the seeds.

2 Soak the #1 peppers in salt water and drain.

3 Mix the beef and bean curd with the seasoning.

4 Dip the inside of the peppers into flour. Stuff them with the #3 mixture and dip them into flour again.

5 Dip the stuffed peppers into beaten egg and fry until golden brown.

Mung Bean Pancake
Pindaettŏk (빈대떡)

Ingredients   1 cup dried mung beans, ⅓ cup rice, ½ cup water, 1 oz. pork, ginger, 1 clove garlic, sesame oil, MSG, 1 oz. kimchi, red pepper thread, 2 green onions, cherry, parsley

Method   **1** Soak the mung beans several hours in water and rub off the skins. Grind soaked rice and the mung beans with water in a blender.

2 Cut the pork into thin strips and mix it with the chopped garlic, ginger and seasoning.

3 Squeeze the water from the kimchi. Cut it into thin strips and mix it with sesame oil.

4 Drop the **#1** batter by tablespoonfuls onto a hot oiled pan and top it evenly with the vegetable and pork strips. Fry until golden brown.

Hint   It tastes better to fry the batter in pork fat instead of oil.

1 Grind the soaked rice and mung beans with water in a blender.

3 Cut the pork into thin strips and season.

2 Squeeze the water from the kimchi. Cut it into thin strips and mix it with sesame oil.

4 Drop the batter onto a greased pan and top with the kimchi, pork, green onion and red pepper thread.

Fried Green Onion
P'ajŏn (파전)

Ingredients ¼ lb. small green onion, ¼ bundle watercress, 1 oż. pork, ½ cup sea mussel, ½ cup rice powder, 1 egg, salt, vinegar-soy sauce, lettuce

Method **1** Trim the small green onions and watercress and cut them into 4″ lengths.

2 Slice the pork thinly and chop the sea mussel finely.

3 Add a little water to the rice flour and a little salt and mix into a light batter.

4 Spread the sliced green onions in an oiled pan and place the sliced watercress between the green onion slices.

5 Arrange the pork and sea mussel evenly on the **#4** vegetables. Spread the **#3** batter on the top and cook slightly. Then cover the top with beaten egg and fry until golden brown. Serve with vinegar-soy sauce for dipping.

1 Cut the small green onions and watercress into 4″ lengths.

2 Chop the sea mussel and slice the pork thinly.

3 Mix the rice flour, salt and a little water into a light batter.

4 Place the **#1**, **#2** ingredients in an oiled pan and spread the **#3** batter on the top.

5 When the **#4** patty gets cooked slightly, cover it with beaten egg and fry.

Fried Zucchini
Hobakchŏn (호박전)

1 Cut the young zucchini into ¼" thick circles.

4 Dry the squash slices and dip them into flour and top them with the **#3** mixture evenly.

5 Cover the zucchini slices with beaten egg and fry until golden brown.

2 Sprinkle the squash slices with the salt.

3 Mix the minced beef and mashed bean curd with the seasoning.

Ingredients   1 zucchini, 2 oz. beef, 1 egg, ½ cake bean curd, 1 green onion, 1 clove garlic, ¼ cup flour, 4 tbsp. salt, 1 red pepper

Method   **1** Cut the zucchini into ¼" thick circles and sprinkle it with the salt.

2 Mince the beef finely.

3 Mix the mashed bean curd, minced beef and beaten egg with the seasoning.

4 Dry the squash slices and dip them into flour. Spoon the **#3** mixture on the center of the squash slice. Then dip them into flour and into beaten egg and fry until golden brown.

5 Decorate with the red pepper and serve with the seasoning sauce.

Fried Zucchini

Skewered Garlic
Manŭl Sanjŏk (마늘 산적)

Ingredients   40 cloves garlic, 2 oz. ham, 1 carrot, 1 cucumber, 2 tbsp. soy sauce, sesame oil, MSG, 2 eggs, ½ cup flour, parsley, skewers

Method   **1** Scald the garlic slightly in hot salt water.

2 Cut the ham, cucumber and carrot into the same size as the garlic and season them with the soy sauce, sesame oil and MSG.

3 On skewers, string the garlic, ham, cucumber and carrot slices in order and dip the under side of the skewered food into flour.

4 Dip the skewered food into beaten egg and fry in a greased pan.

Skewered Garlic

1 Scald the garlic briefly in salt water.

2 Cut the ham, cucumber and carrot into the same size as the garlic.

3 Season the **#1**, **#2** ingredients with the soy sauce, sesame oil and MSG.

4 Dip the under side of the skewered food into flour and dip them into beaten egg and fry.

Skewered Fish
Ŏsanjŏk (어산적)

1 Mince the beef finely and season.

3 Season the fish pieces with the salt, sesame oil and MSG.

5 Fill the space with the seasoned beef.

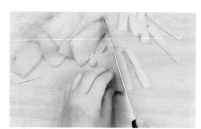

2 Slice thinly and then cut the butterfish into 2¾″ lengths.

4 Skewer #3 leaving space between each one to stuff with the beef.

6 Pound the skewered food with the back of a knife gently and fry.

Ingredients **A** ¼ lb. beef, ½ tbsp. soy sauce, 1 tsp. sugar, 1 tsp. sesame oil, sesame salt, black pepper, green onion, garlic
B 2 butterfish, ½ tbsp. salt, 1 tsp. sesame oil, MSG
C 1 bundle parsley, 6 cherries, pine nut powder
Method **1** Mince the beef finely and season it with the **A** ingredients.
2 Remove the head, tail and entrails from the butterfish and skin it. Slice thinly and cut the fish into ¼″ thick and 2¾″ long rectangles.
3 Season the fish pieces with the salt, sesame oil and MSG. Skewer the fish pieces leaving space between each one to be filled with the meat.
4 Fill the space with the seasoned beef, pound the skewered food with the back of a knife to tenderize and fry in a fry pan.
5 Serve the fried skewered food garnished with parsley and cherry on a plate.

126

Vegetable Salads
Cold Vegetable Dishes
Raw Salads

Mung Bean Sprout Salad
Sukchunamul（숙주나물）

Bracken Salad
Kosarinamul（고사리나물）

Ingredients   ½ lb. mung bean sprouts, 1 tbsp. soy sauce, 1 tbsp. chopped garlic, 1 tbsp. sesame salt, 2 tsp. salt, 2 tsp. sesame oil, sesame seed, MSG, red pepper thread

Method   **1** Clean the mung bean sprouts, scald them in boiling salted water and drain.

2 Sprinkle the seasoning sauce on the scalded mung bean sprouts and mix well. Top them with the red pepper threads and sesame seed and serve.

1 Scald the mung bean sprouts in boiling salted water.

2 Mix the seasoning to make the seasoning sauce.

3 Sprinkle the seasoning sauce on the scalded mung bean sprouts and mix well.

Ingredients   ½ lb. bracken, salt, 1 tsp. soy sauce, 1 tsp. sugar, 1 tbsp. chopped garlic, 1 tbsp. sesame oil, 1 tbsp. sesame salt, 2 tbsp. oil, MSG

Method   **1** Soak the bracken in water and remove the tough stems. Cut into 4" lengths and squeeze out the water.

2 Stir-fry the bracken in an oiled pan sprinkling it with the sesame salt, chopped garlic, sesame oil, MSG, salt and soy sauce.

1 Soak the bracken in water and remove the tough stems. Cut it into 4" lengths.

2 Stir-fry the bracken in an oiled pan.

3 Season to taste.

Mung Bean Sprout Salad

Seasoned Dried Pollack
Pugŏmuch'im (북어무침)

Ingredients   **A** 1 dried pollack
B 1 tsp. sugar, 1 tsp. salt, ½ tsp. sesame oil, 1 tsp. sesame salt
C 1 tsp. sugar, 1 tsp. salt, ½ tsp. sesame oil, 1 tsp. sesame salt, 1 tsp. red pepper powder, 3 tbsp. salad oil
D 1 tsp. sugar, 1 tsp. sesame salt, ½ tsp. sesame oil

Method   **1** Pound the dried pollack with a wooden mallet and peel. Remove the dried flesh from

the bones and head.
2 Shred the flesh finely and wrap it in a damp cloth to soften.
3 Pound the wrapped flesh in a mortar to fluff it up.
4 Rub the **#3** flesh with your hands to soften.
5 Divide the shredded flesh into three equal parts. Mix the **B, C** and **D** ingredients separately with one-third the flesh to make three

colors. When mixing the **C** ingredients add some red pepper oil.

Hint   Buy yellow dried pollack. You may pound the dried pollack with a mallet or use the dried pollack slices.

Bracken Salad

1 Pound the dried pollack with a mallet.

3 Rub the **#2** flesh with your hands to fluff it up.

2 Shred the flesh finely and wrap it in a damp cloth. Pound the wrapped flesh with a mallet in a mortar.

4 Mix the flesh (divided into three equal parts) separately with the three seasonings— **B, C, D.**

129

Garland Chrysanthemum Salad Jellied Mung-Bean Puree

Ssukkatmuch'im (쑥갓무침)

Ch'ongp'omuch'im (청포무침)

Ingredients 1 bundle garland chrysanthemum, ½ tbsp. soy sauce, ½ tbsp. salt, green onion, garlic, sesame oil, sesame salt

Method 1 Trim the garland chrysanthemum and remove any tough stems.

2 Scald the garland chrysanthemum in boiling salted water. Rinse it in cold water and drain.

3 Squeeze the water from the scalded garland chrysanthemum and season it with the chopped green onion and garlic.

1 Scald the garland chrysanthemum (starting with the stems) in boiling salted water and rinse it in cold water.

2 Season with the soy sauce, sesame salt, garlic, green onion, red pepper thread and sesame oil.

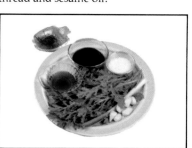

Jellied Mung-Bean Puree

Ingredients 2 cakes jellied mung-bean, ½ carrot, 1 cucumber, 2 oz. kimchi, 4 oz. soy bean sprouts, 1 egg, 1 oz. green bell pepper, ½ tsp. soy sauce, 1 tsp. salt, 1 tbsp. vinegar, 1 tbsp. sugar, ½ tbsp. sesame salt, sesame oil

Method 1 Cut the jellied mung-bean puree into ¼" thick strips and mix it with the sesame oil and salt. Squeeze the water from the kimchi and cut it into thin strips. Mix it with the sesame oil and sugar.

2 Cut the beef into thin strips and season it with the green onion, garlic, soy sauce, sugar, sesame salt and black pepper. Fry and cool it. Cut the carrot into thin strips and fry it with salt slightly.

3 Remove the hairlike roots from the bean sprouts. Scald the sprouts

Todok Salad
Tŏdŏkmuch'im (더덕무침)

Ingredients   ¼ lb. todok (a white root), ½ bundle watercress, 1 tbsp. red pepper paste, 1 tbsp. vinegar, 1 tbsp. sugar, green onion, garlic, sesame oil, sesame salt, lettuce

Method   1 Pound the todok with a mallet and wash by rubbing it with your hands in salt water. Shred it finely and squeeze out the water.

2 Cut the watercress into 2″ lengths.

3 Mix the todok and watercress with the vinegar-red pepper paste. Serve the todok salad on lettuce leaves.

Hint   Todok loses its puckery taste if rubbed in salt water. Todok salad, seasoned with vinegar and sugar, will stimulate your appetite. Todok is a low calorie food.

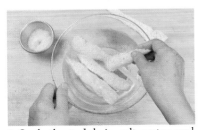

1 Soak the todok in salt water and drain.

2 Shred the todok finely.

3 Mix the todok and watercress with the vinegar-red pepper paste.

in salted water, drain and mix them with the sesame oil.

4 Remove the seeds from the bell pepper and red pepper and cut them into thin strips.

5 Cut the cucumber into thin strips and sprinkle it with salt. Squeeze out the water and fry lightly. Fry the beaten egg into a thin sheet and cut it into thin strips.

6 Mix all the ingredients with the vinegar-soy sauce. Sprinkle with the powdered laver and serve.

1 Cut the jellied mung-bean puree into thick strips and mix it with the sesame oil and salt.

3 Cut the carrot into thin strips, fry it lightly and salt it.

2 Remove the hairlike roots from the bean sprouts. Scald them and mix with the sesame oil.

4 Mix the jellied mung-bean puree, bean sprouts, cucumber and carrot strips with the vinegar-soy sauce.

131

Seasoned Cucumber with Vinegar
Oich'omuch'im（오이초무침）

Ginseng Rootlet Salad
Misammuch'im（미삼무침）

1 Soak the cucumber and radish slices in the vinegar-water.

2 Drain and mix the marinated vegetables with the lemon pieces.

3 Sprinkle with the sesame seed and red pepper thread.

Ginseng Rootlet Salad

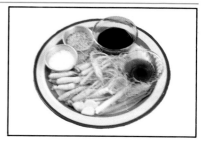

1 Clean and drain the rootlets of ginseng.

Ingredients   ½ lb. rootlets of ginseng, salt, 1 tbsp. soy sauce, 2 tsp. sugar, green onion, garlic, ½ tbsp. sesame salt, 1 tsp. sesame oil
Method   **1** Wash the rootlets

of ginseng until clean and drain.
2 Steam the rootlets of ginseng on a damp cloth in a steamer and place them in a wicker tray.
3 Mix the chopped green onion

and garlic with the seasonings to make the sauce.
4 Mix the steamed rootlets with the seasoning sauce.
Hint   Even if you mix the root-

132

Fresh Seaweed with Vinegar
Saengmiyŏk Ch'och'ae (생미역 초채)

Ingredients 2 cucumbers, ¼ white Korean radish, ½ lemon, vinegar, 2 tbsp. sugar, 1 tbsp. salt, 1 tsp. sesame seed, red pepper thread

Method **1** Clean the cucumbers by rubbing them with salt and drain. Cut them into slices 2″ long. Sprinkle with salt and allow them to stand. Squeeze out the water.

2 Cut the radish into the same size as the cucumber slices.

3 Cut the lemon into ginko leaf-shaped pieces.

4 Combine the salt, vinegar and sugar to make the sauce. Sprinkle the cucumber and radish slices with the sauce and let them stand.

5 Mix the lemon and marinated vegetable slices.

6 Sprinkle the sesame seed and red pepper thread on the mixture and serve with the seasoning sauce; 2 tbsp. vinegar, 1 tbsp. sugar and 1 tsp. soy sauce.

Hint Place the cucumber in a dry cloth and squeeze out the water by pressing it down gently.

2 Steam the rootlets of ginseng in a steamer.

3 Mix the steamed rootlets with the seasoning sauce.

lets of ginseng with a vinegar-red pepper paste, the fragrance of ginseng will prevail and stimulate your appetite.

Ingredients ⅓ lb. fresh brown seaweed, ¼ lb. crab meat jelly, ½ cucumber, 1 tbsp. vinegar, 1 tbsp. red pepper powder, 1 clove garlic, 2 tsp. salt, 1 tbsp. sugar, ½ tsp. sesame salt

Method **1** Clean the fresh seaweed and scald it in boiling water for 3 minutes. Rinse it in cold water and cut it into small pieces.

1 Clean the fresh seaweed and scald it in boiling water for 3 minutes.

2 Rinse the scalded seaweed in cold water and cut it into small pieces.

2 Halve the cucumber and cut it into half-circles. Sprinkle them with the salt and squeeze out the water.

3 Shred the crab meat jelly.

4 Mix the seaweed, cucumber pieces and crab meat jelly with the red pepper powder, garlic, sesame salt, vinegar and sugar.

Hint You may cook the fresh seaweed as it is without scalding.

3 Shred the crab meat jelly.

4 Mix the seaweed, crab meat jelly and cucumber pieces with the seasoning.

Bellflower Root Salad
Toraji Saengch'ae (도라지 생채)

White Radish Salad
Muu Saengch'ae (무우 생채)

Ingredients   ½ lb. bellflower roots, ½ cucumber, 2 tbsp. red pepper powder, 2 cloves garlic, 1 tbsp. chopped green onion, 1½ tbsp. sugar, 1 tsp. salt, ½ tsp. soy sauce, 1 tbsp. vinegar

Method   **1** Shred the bellflower roots finely using a toothpick.

2 Clean the shredded bellflower by rubbing it with the salt. Squeeze out the water.

3 Cut the cucumber into half-circles. Sprinkle with salt and squeeze out the water.

4 Mix the bellflower roots and cucumber pieces with the seasoning and vinegar.

Hint   Rub the bellflower roots with salt to remove the bitterness. Squeeze the cucumber tightly.

1 Shred the bellflower roots using a toothpick.

2 Rub the shredded bellflower with salt.

3 Squeeze out the water and season.

Ingredients   ½ lb. white Korean radish, ½ tbsp. red pepper powder, 1 tsp. salt, 1 tbsp. sugar, 1 green onion, 1 clove garlic, vinegar, lettuce

Method   **1** Peel the radish and cut it into 2" long, thin strips.

2 Mix the radish strips with the red pepper powder.

3 Add the sugar, salt, red pepper threads, green onion and chopped garlic to the **#2** mixture.

4 Sprinkle the **#3** mixture with the vinegar and mix well.

Hint   Sprinkle the radish with salt and squeeze out the water, then season it once again to taste.

White Radish Salad

Cold Cooked Jellyfish
Haep'ari Naengch'ae (해파리 냉채)

1 Cut the carrot, cucumber, egg sheets and jellyfish into thin strips.

2 Mix the radish strips with the red pepper powder first.

3 Make the garlic sauce.

Ingredients   **A** ⅔ lb. jellyfish, 1 cucumber, ½ carrot, 1 egg
B 3 cloves garlic, ¼ cup water, 1 tbsp. vinegar, ½ tsp. salt, 1 tsp. sugar, ½ tsp. soy sauce, ½ tsp. sesame oil
C 3½ tbsp. dry mustard, 1½ tbsp. sugar, 1 tbsp. salt, ½ tbsp. soy sauce, ¼ cup vinegar, ¼ cup water

Method   **1** Buy tender jellyfish and soak it in cold water to remove the salt water, then scald it in water at 140°F.
2 Cut the scalded jellyfish into thin strips and marinate it in the sugar and vinegar.
3 Cut the cucumber and carrot into thin strips.

4 Fry the beaten egg yolk and white separately into thin sheets and cut them into thin strips.
5 Mix the chopped garlic with the **B** ingredients to make the garlic sauce.
6 Mix the mustard with the **C** ingredients to make the mustard sauce.
7 Mix the **#2** jellyfish and cucumber strips. Place the mixture in the center of a plate and surround it with alternating spokes of the egg, carrot and cucumber strips.
8 Serve with the garlic sauce and the mustard sauce.
Hint   If you scald the jellyfish in water hotter than 160°F it becomes tough.

1 Cut the radish into 2″ long, thin strips.

2 Mix the **#1** ingredients with the vinegar and sugar.

3 Add the remaining seasonings and mix well.

Mustard Salad
Kyŏjach'ae (겨자채)

1 Place the bowl containing the mustard paste face down on a hot pot and let it stand.

2 Cut the ham into thin strips.

3 Cut the cucumber, carrot and egg sheet into thin strips.

4 Score the squid diagonally and cut it into thin strips.

5 Grind the pine nuts in a mortar adding the mustard-vinegar sauce.

Ingredients   ¼ lb. ham, 1 cucumber, ¼ pear, ½ carrot, 1 squid, ¼ lb. jellyfish, 5 chestnuts, 1 egg, 7 tbsp. dry mustard, 3 tbsp. pine nuts, 1 tbsp. soy sauce, 3 tbsp. sugar, 2 tbsp. salt, ½ cup vinegar, ½ cup water

Method   **1** Cut the ham into thin strips.

2 Cut the cucumber, carrot and egg sheets into the same strips as the ham.

3 Peel and cut the pear into thin strips. Soak it in sugar water.

4 Slice the chestnuts thinly.

5 Halve the squid. Score it crosswise and lengthwise at ¼" intervals and cut it into thin strips. Scald and cool.

6 Rinse the jellyfish three times to remove the salt water and scald it in water at 140°F. Cut it into thin strips and mix it with the vinegar and sugar.

7 Slowly stir boiling water into the mustard; stir until a smooth paste forms in the bowl. Put the bowl containing the mustard paste face down on a hot pot and let it stand for 10-15 minutes. When the mustard is complete, add the soy sauce, sugar, vinegar, water and salt and mix well. Grind the pine nuts in a mortar adding the above mustard mixture to make the mustard-vinegar sauce.

8 Arrange the prepared vegetables attractively around the mustard-vinegar sauce.

Hint   **1** After removing the tops from the pine nuts, grind the pine nuts in a mortar, so that they do not float on top of the mustard-vinegar sauce.

2 You may use boiled beef, pork or chicken instead of the ham.

5-Color Bean Sprout Dish

K'ongnamul Osaekch'ae (콩나물 오색채)

Ingredients ½ bundle watercress, ½ cup water, ½ carrot, 1½ tsp. salt, ½ lb. bean sprouts, 1 egg, 2 oz. beef, 3 dried brown, oak mushrooms, ½ round onion, 1 tsp. sesame oil, 1 green onion, black pepper, MSG

Method **1** Place the trimmed bean sprouts (without the hairlike roots) with ½ cup water and 1 tsp. salt in a covered pan and bring to a boil. When cooked, mix them with the sesame oil.

2 Cut the carrot into thin strips and stir-fry with salt.
3 Cut the watercress into 2″ lengths and stir-fry with salt.
4 Fry the beaten egg into a sheet and cut it into thin strips.
5 Cut the beef, dried mushrooms and round onion into thin strips, season and fry.
6 Arrange the bean sprouts, carrot, watercress and egg strips in circles around the beef-mushroom mixture in the center of the plate.

1 Boil the bean sprouts with the salt and water.

3 Cut the egg sheet, carrot and watercress into thin strips.

2 Mix the boiled bean sprouts with the sesame oil.

4 Fry the beef, dried mushroom and round onion strips.

Sliced Raw Skate

Hongŏhoe (홍어회)

Ingredients   1 skate, ½ Korean hard pear, ½ white Korean radish, ½ bundle watercress, 2 green peppers, pine nuts, lettuce, 4 tbsp. red pepper paste, 7 tbsp. vinegar, 1 tbsp. sugar, 1 tbsp. sesame salt, 1 tsp. sesame oil, 1 green onion, 4 cloves garlic, MSG, 1 tbsp. red pepper powder, 2 red peppers

Method   **1** Skin and cut the skate diagonally into bite-sized pieces. Sprinkle with 4 tbsp. vinegar and let them stand. Then squeeze out the water.

2 Cut the radish and pear into the same size as the skate pieces. Sprinkle the radish with the salt, vinegar and sugar and squeeze out the water. Soak the pear in sugar water and drain.

3 Cut the watercress, red peppers and green peppers into the same size as the skate pieces.

4 Combine the **#1**, **#2** and **#3** ingredients well with the seasonings.

5 Place the **#4** mixture on lettuce leaves on a plate and sprinkle the top with the pine nuts.

Ingredients   ½ lb. tuna, 1 butterfish, 2 abalones, 1 squid, 1 laver, 5 blood clams, ¼ cucumber, 3 cherries, 2 lettuce leaves, 1 piece turnip, 1 piece carrot, 1 tbsp. lemon juice, 2 tbsp. red pepper paste, 1 clove garlic, 1 green onion, 1 tsp. sesame salt, 1 tsp. sesame oil

Method   **1** Slice the tuna thinly and cut it into bite-sized pieces.

2 Skin the butterfish and remove the entrails. Slice the flesh into bite-sized pieces.

3 Clean the abalones by rubbing them with salt and removing the entrails and shells. Slice the abalone flesh thinly and place the slices in the shells.

4 Remove the entrails, head and

1 Sprinkle the sliced skate with the vinegar and squeeze out the water.

3 Sprinkle the radish pieces with the vinegar, sugar and salt and squeeze out the water.

1 Slice the tuna thinly and cut it into bite-sized pieces.

2 Cut the pear and radish into the same size as the skate pieces. Soak the pear pieces in sugar water and drain.

4 Combine the **#1**, **#2** and **#3** ingredients thoroughly with the seasoned red pepper paste.

legs from the squid and skin it. Score the body of the squid at ¼″ intervals.

5 Spread the sheet of laver on the inside of the squid, roll it up and wrap it firmly. Cut the roll into bite-sized rings.

6 Remove the flesh from the shells of the blood clams. Clean it and cut it into bite-sized pieces.

7 Arrange the prepared ingredients on a layer of shredded white radish and garnish with the cucumber, cherries and flower-shaped carrots.

8 Serve with the vinegar-red pepper paste.

2 Slice the flesh of abalone thinly and place it in the shell.

3 Skin and score the squid.

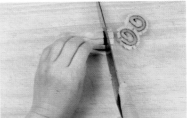

4 Place the sheet of laver on the body of the squid, roll it up and cut it into slices.

Ingredients   1 bundle small green onion, 2 eggs, ½ lb. ham, 2 tbsp. pine nut, red pepper thread, 1 tbsp. red pepper paste, 1 tbsp. sugar, 1 tsp. chopped green onion, 1 tsp. chopped garlic, 1 tbsp. vinegar, pine nut powder

Method   **1** Scald the small green onions (starting with the stems) in salted water.

2 Fry the beaten egg yolk and white separately into thick sheets and cut them into pieces ⅓″ × 1⅔″. Cut the ham into the same size as the egg.

4 Arrange the egg white, ham and yolk in order and place red pepper threads and pine nuts on the top. Then tie them with the small green onion to make a bundle.

5 Serve the #4 bundles with the vinegar-red pepper paste sauce sprinkled with powdered pine nuts for dipping.

Green Onion Bundles

Watercress Bundles
Minariganghoe (미나리강회)

1 Scald the watercress stems in boiling salted water and rinse them in cold water.

2 Skin the squid and score it diagonally. Cut into thick strips and scald it in boiling salted water.

3 Tie the squid strips with the scalded watercress stems to make a bundle.

Ingredients 2 bundles watercress, 1 squid, 2 tbsp. red pepper paste, 1 tbsp. vinegar, 1 tbsp. sugar, 1 tbsp. powdered pine nuts

Method **1** Remove the leaves from the watercress and clean. Parboil the stems in boiling salted water and rinse them in cold water.

2 Skin the body of the squid and score it diagonally at ¼″ intervals. Cut into thick strips and scald it in boiling salted water. Mix the seasonings to make the seasoned red pepper paste.

3 Place the red pepper thread on the squid strips and tie them with the scalded watercress to make a bundle. Serve the bundles with the seasoned red pepper paste for dipping.

1 Scald the small green onions (starting with the stems) in salted water.

2 Cut the ham and egg sheets into pieces ⅓″ × 1⅔″

3 Arrange #2, red pepper thread and pine nut in order. Then tie them with the small green onion to make a bundle.

Snacks
Basic Side Dishes

Egg Dishes
Bean Curd Dishes
Bean Cookery

Egg Soup
Talgyalt'ang (달걀탕)

Soft Bean Curd Soup
Sundubutchigae (순두부찌개)

Ingredients   2 eggs, ⅓ lb. beef, various seasoning, 2 dried brown, oak mushrooms, 2 small green onions, 5 cups water, 1 tbsp. nicely aged soy sauce, salt, black pepper, MSG

Method   **1** Soak the dried mushrooms in water, remove the stems and cut them into thin strips.

1 Season the beef and dried mushroom strips.

2 Add the small green onion and beaten egg and stir slightly.

2 Cut the beef into thin strips. Season the beef and dried mushrooms.

3 Trim the small green onions and cut them into 2″ lengths.

4 Beat the eggs slightly.

5 Fry the beef and dried mushrooms in a soup pot. Add the water and bring to a boil. Add the small green onion and beaten egg

to the boiling broth stirring slightly. Check the seasoning and serve.

Hint   Instead of stirring egg into the soup, place the bowl containing the seasoned beaten egg in boiling water and cook until set. Cut the cooked egg into bite-sized pieces and add it to the soup with the garland chrysanthemum leaves.

Soft Bean Curd Soup

Ingredients   3 cups soft bean curd, ½ cup clam meat, ¼ lb. pork, 1 green onion, 4 cloves garlic, soy sauce, 3 tbsp. red pepper powder, beef suet, black pepper, 1½ cup water

Method   **1** Stir-fry the red pepper powder with oil in a pan to make the red pepper oil.

2 Cut the pork into thin strips. Trim the clams and remove the entrails.

3 Add the pork strips and garlic to the red pepper oil and fry together. Season with the soy sauce and add 1½ cup water.

4 When the **#3** soup boils, add the soft bean curd. Bring to a boil again and add the clam meat and green onion cut diagonally.

Hint   How to make soft bean curd: [Ingredients] 1 cup yellow soy beans soaked in water, 5 cups

Seasoned Fermented Soybean Soup
Ch'ŏnggukchangtchigae (청국장찌개)

1 Fry the red pepper powder with oil to make the red pepper oil.

2 Add the pork and garlic to the red pepper oil and fry.

3 When the #2 mixture boils, add the soft bean curd.

4 Add the clam meat and green onion slices.

water, 1 tbsp. brine for curdling [Method] Soak the beans overnight; rub with hands to remove loose skins; drain. Add 5 cups water, grind the beans in a blender and strain. Boil the strained bean liquid in a pot and let it cool to 180°F. Then add the curdling brine. An Epsom salts solution may be used as a curdling agent. Stir the liquid gently three or four times, so that it forms soft curds.

Ingredients 1 cake bean curd, ¼ lb. corbicula clams, 3 dried brown, oak mushrooms, ¼ lb. kimchi, 6-8 tbsp. seasoned fermented soybeans, ¼ lb. beef, 3 cups water, green onion, garlic, soy sauce, red pepper powder, MSG, red peppers, green peppers

Method 1 Cut the bean curd into large pieces. Slice the dried mushrooms, beef and kimchi into thin strips. Mix them with the green onion, garlic and soy sauce and stir-fry. Bring the water to a boil and dissolve the fermented soybeans in it.

2 When the soup boils hard, add the green onion, bean curd pieces and clam meat. Check the seasoning and bring to a boil again.

1 Mix the beef, dried mushroom and kimchi strips with the green onion, garlic and soy sauce and fry.

2 When the #1 mixture boils, dissolve the fermented soybeans in the boiling soup.

3 When the soup boils hard, add the green onion, bean curd pieces and clam meat.

Royal Soybean Paste Soup
Kungjungdoenjangtchigae (궁중된장찌개)

Ingredients ½ lb. minced beef, 1 clove garlic, sesame salt, 2 tbsp. chopped green onion, 1 tsp. sesame oil, black pepper, 12 gingko nuts, 4 skewers, ½ round onion, 3 dried brown, oak mushrooms, 1 green pepper, 1 red pepper, 2 tbsp. soybean paste, 1 green onion, ½ cake bean curd, sesame oil, MSG, ginger, 3 cups water

Method 1 Clean the round onion and dried mushrooms and cut them into thick strips.

2 Season the minced beef with the sesame salt, chopped garlic, green onion, sesame oil and black pepper. Shape the seasoned beef into square patties and broil them on a grill or in a fry pan. Cut the broiled patties into bite-sized pieces.

3 Mix the soybean paste, garlic, ginger and sesame oil, stir in 3 cups of water and bring to a boil.

4 When the mixture boils, add the sliced round onion, dried mushroom and beef patties.

5 Stir-fry the gingko nuts with salt in a fry pan, peel off the top-skins and skewer them on a toothpick.

6 Add the red pepper, green pepper and bean curd cut into square pieces to the boiling soup.

Hint Simmer this soybean paste soup on low heat in an unglazed earthenware bowl just before eating for its original taste.

1 Mix the soybean paste with the garlic, ginger and sesame oil, add the water and boil.

2 Shape the seasoned beef into square patties and broil them in a fry pan.

3 Add the sliced round onion, dried mushroom and beef patties to the boiling soup.

Bean Curd Casserole
Tubu Chŏn-gol (두부 전골)

1 Sprinkle the sliced bean curd with salt and fry.

2 Wrap the spinach firmly in a cabbage leaf and slice.

3 Place the seasoned beef and bean curd between the sliced bean curd, dip them into beaten egg and fry.

4 Form the meatballs and skewer them.

5 Place all the ingredients in a shallow pan.

Ingredients **A.** 2 cakes bean curd **B.** ¼ lb. beef, ½ cake bean curd **C.** 2 cabbage leaves, spinach, various seasonings **D.** 1 round onion 2 oz. beef **E.** 2 eggs **F.** 2½ cup meat stock **G.** soy sauce, salt, black pepper, sesame salt, green onion, garlic, sesame oil **H.** flower-shaped carrot slices

Method 1 Slice the cakes of bean curd into pieces ¼" thick; sprinkle lightly with salt and fry.
2 Mince the **B** beef finely and squeeze the water from the bean curd. Mix the beef and bean curd with the seasoning. Shape the mixture into 15 meatballs ⅓" in diameter. Dip one side of the #1 bean curd piece into flour and put

the remaining meat mixture between the bean curd slices. Dip the stuffed bean curd pieces into beaten egg and fry until golden brown. Halve the bean curd "sandwiches".
3 Scald the cabbage leaves and spinach. Squeeze out the water and mix with the seasoning. Wrap the spinach firmly in a cabbage leaf and cut the roll into ¾" thick rings. Hard-boil the egg, peel it and cut it into a flowerlike shape.
4 Boil the **D** beef and slice it thinly. Mix the boiled beef and sliced round onion strips with the **G** seasoning. Layer this in the bottom of a shallow pan. Arrange all other ingredients, pour on the seasoned broth and bring to a boil.

Mixed Vegetables with Egg
Okchayuk (옥자육)

Steamed Egg
Talgyal Yach'aetchim (달걀 야채찜)

Ingredients ¼ lb. beef, 1 round onion, ¼ carrot, ¼ bundle watercress, 2 dried brown, oak mushrooms, 2 Jew's ear mushrooms, 3 eggs, 1 tbsp. soy sauce, ½ tbsp. sesame oil, 1 tsp. sesame salt, 1 tsp. black pepper, 1 tsp. sugar, 1 tbsp. chopped green onion, 2 cloves garlic, MSG, 1 tsp. salt

Method **1** Slice the beef into thin strips with the grain of the meat.

2 Slice the round onion, carrot, and dried mushrooms into thin strips. Cut the watercress into 1¼" lengths.

3 Fry the beef and vegetable strips with the seasoning sauce in a fry pan. Top the fried food with three raw eggs and cover. After the eggs are soft-set, divide the cooked food into three equal parts and serve.

1 Slice the beef and vegetables into thin strips.

2 Fry the **#1** mixture with the seasoning sauce.

3 Top with the raw eggs dividing the food into three equal parts.

Steamed Egg

Ingredients 4 eggs, 5 shrimp, 2 dried brown, oak mushrooms, ½ carrot, 1 tsp. parsley, 1 tsp. salt, 1 tsp. sugar, red pepper threads, 2 tbsp. tiny salted, soused shrimp juice, 4 tbsp. water, 1 tsp. sesame seed

Method **1** Remove the heads from the shrimp; scald the shrimp in boiling water. Then remove the shells leaving the tails intact.

2 Soak the dried mushrooms in water and clean. Squeeze out the water and cut them into thin strips. Cut the carrot into thin strips. Fry them in an oiled pan and season with the salt and sugar to taste.

3 Beat the eggs in an unglazed earthenware bowl or in a small

Wrapped Bean Curd
Tubussamtchim (두부쌈찜)

Ingredients   2 cakes bean curd, ½ lb. beef, ½ carrot, 1 round onion, 4 green peppers, 1 tbsp. chopped green onion, 1 tbsp. chopped garlic, ½ tbsp. sesame salt, ½ tbsp. sesame oil, ½ tbsp. sugar, 1 tbsp. salt, 1 egg, 5 cabbage leaves, 3 tbsp. flour, black pepper, MSG

Method   1 Wrap the bean curd in a cloth and squeeze out the water.

2 Season the minced beef with the soy sauce, garlic, chopped green onion, sesame salt, sugar, sesame oil, black pepper, and MSG and mix well.

3 Cut the carrot, round onion and green peppers into thin strips and fry them separately in an oiled pan salting each lightly.

4 Mix the #1, #2, #3 ingredients and the egg with the seasonings.

5 Scald the cabbage leaves and dry off the moisture. Sprinkle the insides of the cabbage leaves with flour and then place the #4 mixture on each leaf; roll it up as you would a jelly-roll.

6 Place the rolls on a damp cloth in a steamer and steam.

Hint   You need to regulate the quantity of the water in the steamer and leave a 1¼″ space between the water and the food in order to steam the rolls well.

1 Mix the bean curd, minced beef, fried vegetables and an egg with the seasoning.

2 Place the #1 mixture on each cabbage leaf and roll it firmly.

pot and season them with the sugar, water, salt and salted shrimp juice and stir well.

4 Add the dried mushroom, carrot strips and shrimp to the beaten egg and steam over medium heat for 20 minutes.

5 When half-steamed, top the mixture with the red pepper threads and chopped parsley.

6 Serve in the cooking bowl as is.

Hint   1 You may steam the bowl of egg mixture in a rice kettle, when you boil the rice, on top of the rice.

2 It is better to season the steamed egg with salt, not with soy sauce.

3 You may add minced beef instead of the shrimp or vegetables.

1 Fry the carrot and dried mushroom strips sprinkling them lightly with salt.

2 Beat the eggs well and season.

3 Add the carrot and dried mushroom strips to the beaten egg and steam for 20 minutes.

Stuffed Bean Curd
Tubusobagi (두부소박이)

Steamed Bean Curd
Tubusŏn (두부선)

Ingredients   2 cakes bean curd, ¼ lb. beef, 2 green onions, ½ carrot, 3 stone mushrooms, 5 dried brown, oak mushrooms, 1 egg, 3 quail eggs, ½ tbsp. salt, 1 tbsp. chopped green onion, 1 tbsp. chopped garlic, ½ tbsp. sesame salt, ½ tbsp. sesame oil, 1 tbsp. cornstarch powder, black pepper, MSG

Method   **1** Cut the bean curd into pieces 1¼" thick by 1⅔" × 2" and sprinkle it with salt. Fry the sliced bean curd until golden brown on both sides. Make a D-shaped cut on the top of each piece, lifting out the top slice to replace later. Scoop out the inside.
2 Mince the beef finely and season it with the chopped green onion, garlic, sesame salt, sesame oil, black pepper, MSG and mix well. Soak the stone mushrooms and dried mushrooms in water, clean and cut them into thin strips.
3 Cut the green onions into thin strips. Cut the carrot into thin strips and chop finely. Hard-boil the quail eggs, peel and slice them in two or three equal parts.
4 Combine the minced beef, stone mushroom, dried mushroom, carrot, green onion strips and quail eggs with the sesame oil, sesame salt, black pepper, MSG, salt and starch powder to make the stuffing.
5 Stuff the bean curd with the above mixture. Dip the stuffed bean curd into cornstarch powder, then into beaten egg and replace the lid piece. Brown them lightly in a fry pan. Place the fried bean curd on a damp cloth in a steamer and steam 15 minutes. Halve the steamed pieces and serve.

1 Fry the bean curd pieces until golden brown on both sides.

3 Stuff the pieces with the stuffing and dip them into cornstarch powder.

2 Score one side of each piece into a "D" form to make the lid and scoop out the inside.

4 Steam the stuffed bean curd for 15 minutes and cut into halves.

Ingredients   ⅔ lb. bean curd, ¼ lb. minced beef, 5 dried brown, oak mushrooms, 5 stone mushrooms, 1 egg, 1 tsp. pine nuts, red pepper threads, 2 tsp. salt, 1 tbsp. chopped green onion, ½ tbsp. chopped garlic, 1 tsp. sesame oil, black pepper, water, 1 tsp. sugar

Method   **1** Mix the minced beef and mashed bean curd well with the seasoning and shape the mixture into a square patty.

2 Soak the stone mushrooms and dried mushrooms in water and cut them into thin strips. Fry the beaten egg yolk and egg white separately into sheets and cut them into thin strips. Halve the pine nuts.

3 Place the #1 patty on a damp cloth in a steamer and top it with the #2 prepared garnish and steam.
4 When the steamed patty cools, cut it into bite-sized pieces and serve with the vinegar-soy sauce.

Steamed Bean Curd

1 Mix the mashed bean curd and minced beef well with the seasoning.

2 Place the square patty in a steamer, top it with the garnish and steam.

Ingredients 5 eggs, 1 tbsp. salt, ¼ cup soy sauce, 1 tbsp. sugar, ⅔ cup water, 1 tsp. ginger juice, lettuce leaves

Method **1** Hard-boil the eggs in salted water for 12 minutes.

2 Rinse the boiled eggs in cold water and peel.

3 Simmer the peeled eggs with ⅔ cup water, ¼ cup soy sauce, 1 tbsp. sugar and ginger juice in a pot. When the liquid is almost evap-

orated, cook them on high heat until glazed.

4 Cool the eggs and cut them into bite-sized pieces. Serve on a platter with lettuce leaves and parsley.

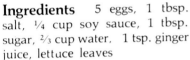

1 Hard-boil the eggs.

2 Rinse the eggs in cold water and peel.

Bean Curd in Soy Sauce
Tubut'wigimjorim (두부튀김조림)

Salted Bean Curd and Beef
Tubu Soegogijorim (두부 쇠고기조림)

Ingredients 2 cakes bean curd, 2 tbsp. salt, 5 tbsp. flour, 4 dried brown, oak mushrooms, 4 green peppers, 1 red pepper, 4 pieces fried bean curd, 4 cups broth, 1½ tbsp. sugar, 2 tbsp. rice wine, 2½ tbsp. soy sauce

Method 1 Pat the bean curd until dry with a cloth. Divide the bean curd into 8 equal parts and sprinkle them with salt.
2 Dip the bean curd pieces into flour and deep-fry them in oil on medium heat.
3 Scald the fried bean curd in boiling water, cover them with cold water and cut them into halves.
4 Scald the dried mushrooms slightly, remove the stems and cut them into halves.
5 Trim the stems to ⅓" in length on the green peppers and red pepper.
6 Boil the broth with the sugar, rice wine and soy sauce in a pot. Add the fried bean curd, deep-fried bean curd pieces and dried mushrooms and simmer. Then add the red pepper and green peppers and cook briefly so that the color does not change.

2 Cut the bean curd and dip the pieces into salt and flour.

4 Simmer the deep-fried pieces with the seasoning.

1 Sprinkle the bean curd with salt and gently press out the moisture.

3 Deep-fry the bean curd in oil on medium heat until golden brown.

5 Add the green peppers and cook slightly.

Ingredients 1 cake bean curd, ¼ lb. beef, 2 oz. konyak: jellied potato-cake, 2 oz. carrot, 1 green bell pepper, 2 dried brown, oak mushrooms, 1 tbsp. frying oil, 2 tbsp. rice wine, 3 tbsp. soy sauce, 2 tbsp. sugar, ¾ cup water, ginger juice, black pepper.

Method 1 Cut the bean curd

into piece ¾" × 2". Scald them in boiling salted water and rinse them in cold water.
2 Cut the beef, carrot and jellied potato-cake into pieces ¾" × 2" and ¼" thick.
3 Halve the bell peppers and remove the seeds. Cut them into the same size as the above ingredients.

4 Soak the dried mushrooms in water and cut them into halves.
5 Fry the beef, carrot, dried mushroom and bean curd pieces in an oiled pan, add the water and bring to a boil. When the carrot is done, fry on high heat to finish the cooking. Correct the seasoning and add the bell pepper.

Salted Beans
K'ongjorim (콩조림)

1 Scald the sliced bean curd in salt water.

2 Fry all the ingredients except the bell pepper adding water to boil.

3 When carrot gets cooked, finish the cooking on high heat. Then add the bell pepper, fry lightly and serve.

Ingredients　1 cup black beans, 4 tbsp. soy sauce, 3 tbsp. sugar, 4 cups water, 1 tsp. sesame seed, 1 tsp. sesame oil

Method
1 Wash the black beans and soak them in 4 cups water for 3 hours. Put the beans and the soaking water, 2 tbsp. soy sauce and 1½ tbsp. sugar in a pot and cook.

2 When the beans are tender, add the remaining soy sauce and sugar and simmer gently on medium heat.

3 When the beans are almost cooked, add the sesame oil and sesame seed and cook quickly on high heat until glazed.

Hint　First simmer the beans with half of the seasoning and then add the remaining seasoning and cook quickly on high heat.

1 Boil the soaked black beans in water with the soy sauce and sugar.

2 Add the remaining seasoning and cook.

5-Color Egg Rolls
Talgyal Osaekmari (달걀 오색말이)

Ingredients　5 eggs, 2 oz. carrot, 2 oz. bean sprouts, 2 oz. spinach, 2 sheets laver, 2 oz. dried brown, oak mushrooms, salt, soy sauce, sesame oil, sugar

Method　**1** Beat the whites of two eggs, fry them into a thin sheet, salt lightly and cut into thin strips.

2 Beat three eggs and the two egg yolks with a little salt.

3 Cut the carrot into thin strips, fry it with the sesame oil and season it with the salt.

4 Remove the hairlike roots from the bean sprouts and scald. Trim and scald the spinach. Squeeze out the water. Then mix each vegetable separately with the salt, sesame oil and sugar.

5 Soak the dried mushrooms in water and remove the stems. Cut them into thin strips and fry them with the soy sauce, sugar and sesame oil.

6 Pick any hard specks out of the laver. Place a sheet of laver on the bamboo mat. Then lay half of the carrot, bean sprouts, spinach, white strips and dried mushroom on the laver and roll it up as you would a jelly roll. Fill the other sheets of laver in the same fashion to make the rolls.

7 Fry the **#2** beaten eggs on one side only into a thin sheet in an oiled square pan, place the laver roll on the egg and wrap in the egg sheet cooking it until well-done. Place the egg roll on a mat with a raised half-circle design and press it into a flowerlike shape.

8 Cut the **#7** egg rolls into ¾″ lengths and serve them with the vinegar-soy sauce for dipping.

1 Fry the beaten egg whites into a sheet and cut it into thin strips.

2 Place the carrot, mushroom, egg white strips, bean sprouts and spinach on a sheet of laver and roll it up.

3 Place the laver roll on the egg sheet, roll it in a bamboo mat, press lightly to leave a design, and slice.

Egg and Spinach Rolls
Talgyal Shigŭmch'imari (달걀 시금치말이)

Ingredients 2 eggs, 1 tsp. cornstarch, ½ tbsp. water, ½ lb. spinach, 1 tsp. salt, ½ tsp. sugar, 1 tsp. sesame oil, MSG, 2 tbsp. soy sauce

Method **1** Beat the eggs well.
2 Scald the spinach lightly in boiling salted water and rinse it in cold water. Squeeze out the water and season the spinach with the soy sauce, sugar and sesame oil.
3 Dissolve the cornstarch in ½tbsp. water and mix it with the beaten egg, MSG, sugar and salt.
4 Fry the beaten egg on one side only in a thick square pan. Place the scalded spinach on the egg sheet, roll it up and finish cooking. Make the other rolls in the same way.
5 Place the rolls on a kitchen board and cut them diagonally with a sharp knife. Serve with the soy sauce for dipping.

Hint Do not put too much spinach on the egg sheet, and the rolls will look prettier when cut.

3 Place the seasoned spinach on the egg sheet.

1 Scald the spinach and mix it with the seasonings.

2 Fry the beaten egg in a fry pan.

4 Roll #3 and finish cooking.

Cold Cooked Bean Curd
Tubu Naengch'ae (두부 냉채)

Ingredients 1 cake bean curd, 1 tbsp. salt, 2 oz. ham, 2 oz. jellyfish, 1 cucumber, ½ carrot, 1 egg, ½ firm Korean pear, 3 tbsp. vinegar, 3 tbsp. chopped garlic, 1 tbsp. sugar, 1½ tsp. salt, ½ tsp. sesame oil, 3 tbsp. water, 1½ tsp. soy sauce

Method 1 Cut the bean curd into pieces 2″ thick and sprinkle with salt. Fry the pieces until golden brown and cut them into 2″ long strips.

2 Cut the ham into 2″ long strips.

3 Select a thin, green cucumber. Rub it with salt, clean and cut it into the same size as the ham. Remove the salt water from the jellyfish and scald it slightly in hot water (140°F). Cut it into 2″ long strips and marinate it in the vinegar and sugar.

4 Peel the pear and cut it into the same size as the ham. Soak it in sugar water to keep the color and drain.

5 Mix the bean curd and half of the cucumber and jellyfish strips.

6 Arrange the #5 mixture in the center of a plate and arrange the carrot, ham, cucumber, pear and egg strips around it. Serve with the garlic-vinegar sauce for dipping.

1 Sprinkle the bean curd pieces with salt and fry.

3 Make the garlic-vinegar sauce.

2 Cut all the ingredients into thick strips.

4 Arrange the ingredients attractively on a plate.

Rice
Gruel
Noodles

Bean Sprout Rice
K'ongnamulpap (콩나물밥)

Pine Mushroom Rice
Songibŏsŏtpap (송이버섯밥)

Ingredients   3 cups rice, ⅔ lb. bean sprouts, ¼ lb. beef, various seasonings, 3½ cup water, seasonging sauce

Method   **1** Wash the rice and let it stand for 30 minutes before cooking. Trim and clean the bean sprouts.

2 Boil the bean sprouts in 3 cups salted water. Set aside the bean sprout water to use later for boiling the rice.

3 Cut the beef into thin strips, marinate in various seasonings and stir-fry in an oiled pan.

4 Mix the rice and fried beef and pour in the bean sprout liquid. Then boil the mixture.

5 When the rice boils, put the boiled bean sprouts on top and let them cook until well-steamed.

6 Stir the cooked rice, meat and sprouts lightly and serve in a bowl. By seasoning this mixture well a delicious mixed-rice dish results.

1 Boil the bean sprouts in salted water.

2 Fry the seasoned beef.

3 Bring the rice and fried beef to a boil and then add the bean sprouts.

Ingredients   **A.** 10 pine mushrooms

B. 3 cups rice, 3 cups water, 3 tbsp. rice wine, 1 tbsp. soy sauce, ¼ tsp. salt

C. ½ lb. chicken, 2 tsp. soy sauce, 2 tsp. rice wine

Method   **1** Wash the rice.

2 Peel the pine mushrooms and cut them into four equal parts.

3 Cut the chicken into bite-sized pieces and season with the **C** ingredients.

4 Place the prepared rice, pine mushrooms and seasoned chicken in a pot and stir to mix evenly. Pour the remaining **B** ingredients into the pot and boil the mixture on high heat for 10 minutes. Then reduce the heat and cook 10 minutes more until the rice is well done.

Hint   If you wash the pine mushrooms, they change color. Instead, peel, slice and then cook them.

Pine Mushroom Rice

Bean Sprout Rice

1 Peel the pine mushrooms.

2 Cut the pine mushrooms into four equal parts.

3 Season the chicken with the soy sauce and rice wine.

4 Put the rice in a pot and then add the soy sauce and salt.

5 Add **#2** and **#3** to **#4** and cook.

1 Wash the glutinous rice, rice and sorghum.

Ingredients   2 cups glutinous rice, 2 cups regular rice, 1 cup glutinous sorghum, 1 cup glutinous millet, ½ cup dried black beans, ½ cup dried sweet beans, salt

Method   **1** Wash the regular rice and glutinous rice and drain.
2 Clean the sorghum rubbing it well in one's hands until the rinse water is no longer red.
3 Soak the black beans in water and drain. Rinse the sweet beans, boil and drain setting aside the cooking water for later use.

2 Wash the black beans and boil the sweet beans.

3 Boil all the ingredients, add the millet evenly and cook until well-done.

4 Wash the millet and drain.
5 Mix all the ingredients except the millet. Place the mixture in a pot and cover it with the rice water and sweet bean water, add a little salt and boil.
6 When the rice comes to a boil, add the millet evenly, reduce the fire and cook for 10 minutes more until the rice is well-done.

Hint   Mix the grains and water at the ratio of 1 to 1. Salt may be added up to 1 percent of the rice water.

Vegetables to Mix with Rice
Pibimpap (비빔밥)

F. ½ cake mung bean gelatin, salt, sesame oil **G.** ¼ lb. scalded bellflower roots, 1 tsp. soy sauce, ½ tsp. sesame oil, 1 tsp. sesame salt, 1 tsp. salt **H.** 2 eggs **I.** 2 lettuce leaves, seasoning sauce, 1 tsp. sesame oil

Method   **1** Shred and scald the bellflower roots. Fry them seasoning with the **G** ingredients.

2 Cut the beef into thin strips. Fry it seasoning with the **B** ingredients. Cut the bracken into 2″ lengths. Fry it seasoning with the **C** ingredients.

3 Cut the cucumber into half-moon-shaped pieces and sprinkle it with salt. Squeeze out the moisture, season it with the **E** ingredients and fry lightly.

4 Scald the bean sprouts in ½ cup boiling salted water, drain and mix them with the **C** ingredients. Cut the mung bean gelatin into thin strips and mix it with the **F** ingredients.

5 Wash and cook the rice.

6 Fry the egg until it is soft-set.

7 Serve the prepared vegetables with seasoned red pepper paste, the rice and soup.

1 Scald the bellflower roots and fry them with the sesame oil and salt to taste.

Ingredients   **A.** 2 cups rice, 2 cups water **B.** 2 oz. beef, 1 tbsp. soy sauce, ½ tsp. sesame oil, ½ tsp. sesame salt, green onion, garlic, black pepper **C.** ½ lb. bean sprouts, 1 tsp. salt, 1 tsp. sesame oil, green onion, garlic **D.** ¼ lb. boiled bracken, 1 tsp. soy sauce, ½ tsp. sesame oil, ½ tsp. sesame salt, green onion, garlic **E.** 1 cucumber, 1 tsp. salt, sesame oil

2 Cut the beef into thin strips and fry it with the seasoning.

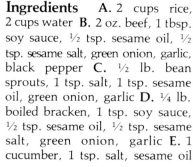

4 Sprinkle the cucumber with salt, squeeze out the moisture and fry lightly.

1 Grind the soaked rice; then add the black sesame seeds and grind again in a blender.

Ingredients   1 cup black sesame seeds, 2 cups rice, 10 cups water, salt, sugar, powdered pine nuts

Method   **1** Clean and soak the black sesame seeds in water. Crush the seeds with a mortar and pestle to remove any hulls. Rinse and stir-fry to dry.

2 Soak and grind the rice with 3 cups water. Add the black sesame

3 Cut the scalded bracken and fry it with the seasoning.

5 Mix the scalded bean sprouts with the sesame oil. Cut the mung bean gelatin into thick strips.

Pine Nut Gruel

Chatchuk (잣죽)

Black Sesame Seed Gruel

Hugimjajuk (흑임자죽)

1 Cut the jujubes into thin strips and marinate them in syrup.

2 Grind the rice in a blender.

3 Boil #1 and #2 stirring well.

Ingredients   2 cups rice, 1 cup pine nuts, 10 cups water, 5 jujubes, salt, sugar syrup

Method   **1** Soak the rice in water and let it stand.

2 Remove the tops from the pine nuts and grind them with 1 cup water in a blender.

3 Pit the jujubes and cut them into thin strips. Marinate them in honey or syrup.

4 Grind the soaked rice with 2 cups water in a blender.

5 Boil the ground rice with the remaining water in a pot. When it gets somewhat thick, add the pine nut liquid slowly stirring as you pour to mix it well and bring the mixture to a boil.

2 Boil the #1 mixture in a pot stirring it well with a wooden spoon.

seeds and grind the mixture again.

3 Boil the #2 mixture with the remaining water on low heat in a thick pan stirring often with a wooden spoon.

Hint   Season the gruel with sugar and salt at the table.

Black Sesame Seed Gruel

Abalone Porridge
Chŏnbokchuk (전복죽)

Ingredients   3 abalones, 1 cup rice, 1 tbsp. sesame oil, 6 cups water, 1 tbsp. salt

Method   **1** Clean the abalones well with a brush, remove the shells and entrails, and cut the abalone meat into thin strips.

2 Grind the soaked rice well in a mortar, add 4 cups water and strain. Save the strained water for later use.

3 Fry the abalone meat with the sesame oil in a heavy pan. Then add the **#2** rice and cook thoroughly.

4 Add the remaining water to **#3** and simmer on low heat until the rice becomes thick. Add the rice-straining water and bring to a boil again.

5 When the porridge comes to a boil, season it with soy sauce and salt to taste.

Hint   **1** If you add the rice-straining water from the start, the porridge will scorch too easily.

2 You must simmer the porridge a long time on low heat because the porridge bubbles over if boiled too quickly on high heat.

1 Cut the abalone meat and grind the rice in a mortar.

2 Add the water to the ground rice and strain.

3 Boil the fried abalones and rice with the water.

4 Add the **#2** rice-straining water and simmer.

Rice-Cake Soup
Ttŏkkuk (떡국)

Ingredients   5 sticks of rice cake, ¼lb. beef, 2 oz. ground beef, 1 egg, 1 tbsp. laver powder, 1 green onion, 1 tbsp. soy sauce, 1 tbsp. chopped green onion, 1 tsp. sesame salt, 1 tsp. chopped garlic, 1 tsp. sesame oil, flour

Method   **1** Leave the soft sticks of rice cake out overnight to harden; cut them diagonally into oval pieces when hard.

2 Cut the beef into thin strips and season.

3 Season and shape the ground beef into meatballs ¾" in diameter. Dip them into flour, then into beaten egg and fry.

4 Fry the beaten egg into a thin sheet and cut it into thin strips.

5 Fry the **#2** beef in a pot and boil it with 8 cups water.

6 When the meat flavor per-

1 Cut the beef into thin strips and fry in an oiled pot.

2 Add the water to **#1** and bring to a boil.

3 When the **#2** soup boils, add the rice cake pieces and boil.

"Ravioli" Soup
P'yŏnsu (편수)

Rice-Cake Soup

meates the broth, add the rice-cake slices and bring to a boil.

7 Season the soup with the soy sauce and salt and add the diagonally cut green onion. Place the rice-cake soup in a bowl and top it with the egg strips, meatballs and powdered laver.

Hint Instead of the egg strips you may add beaten egg to the soup when it is boiling hot.

Ingredients **A.** ¼ lb. beef, ½ cake bean curd, 3 tbsp. beaten egg, ¼ lb. mung bean sprouts, ⅓ zucchini, 2 dried brown, oak mushrooms **B.** 2 tbsp. pine nuts **C.** 6 cups meat stock, 1 tbsp. soy sauce, 1 tsp. salt, MSG **D.** ½ tbsp. soy sauce, ½ tsp. salt, 1 green onion, 3 cloves garlic, 1 tsp. sesame salt, sesame oil, black pepper **E.** 1½ cup flour, 1 tsp. salt, ½ cup warm water **F.** 3 tbsp. soy sauce, 1 tsp. sugar, 2 tsp. vinegar, green onion, garlic, sesame salt

Method **1** Mince the beef finely and fry it in a fry pan.

2 Squeeze the water from the bean curd. Scald and drain the mung bean sprouts, chop them finely and squeeze out the water.

3 Remove the stems from the dried mushrooms and chop them. Cut the zucchini into thin strips and sprinkle it with salt; squeeze out the water and fry lightly.

4 Add the **D** seasonings to #1, #2 and #3 ingredients and mix well.

5 Knead the flour water and salt to make a thick dough. Put the dough into a vinyl bag and let it stand for 30 minutes.

6 Roll the dough into thin sheets and cut them into 2" square pieces. Place the #4 mixture and a pine nut on each square, pinch the four edges together tightly to make the square-shaped "ravioli".

7 Boil the **C** ingredients and add the #6 dumplings. When the soup comes to a boil, add ½ cup cold broth and bring it to a boil again.

8 Top the soup with the egg strips and green onion and serve with the seasoned vinegar sauce.

1 Mix the fried beef and all the ingredients with the seasoning.

2 Place the #1 mixture and a pine nut on each square and pinch the four edges together tightly.

Thin Noodles on a Wicker Tray

Ch'aebansomyŏn (채반소면)

Noodles with Beans

K'ongguksu (콩국수)

Ingredients ⅓ lb. thin noodles, 1 egg, ¼ lb. jellied crab meat, ½ cucumber, 3 stone mushrooms, 2 small green onions, 5 chrysanthemum leaves, 2 tbsp. soy sauce, 1 tbsp. rice wine, 1 tbsp. sugar, black pepper, 3 cups anchovy-kelp broth

Method **1** Boil the thin noodles briefly and rinse them in cold water.

Roll the boiled noodles around the tips of chopsticks and place them on chrysanthemum leaves on a wicker tray.

2 Fry the egg yolk and white separately into sheet and cut them into thin strips. Cut the cucumber into thin strips and shred the jellied crab meat finely.

3 Boil three anchovies and one

piece of kelp with three cups water. Pour the boiled liquid into a bowl and let it cool to make the broth.

4 Add the seasoning to the **#3** broth to make the seasoning sauce.

5 Top the rolls of noodles with the sliced stone mushrooms and arrange them with the **#2** ingredients on a wicker tray. Serve with the seasoning sauce.

1 Roll the noodles around the tips of chopsticks and place them on chrysanthemum leaves on a wicker tray.

2 Cut all the ingredients into thin strips and shred the jellied crab meat.

3 Add the seasoning to the kelp broth to make the seasoning sauce.

Serve with salt.

Ingredients 1 cup dried soybeans, 4 or 5 cups water, ¼ lb. noodles, 1 cucumber, salt, ½ tomato, 1 egg

Method **1** Wash the soybeans and let them stand overnight. Boil for 15 minutes and rinse them in cold water to remove the hulls. Grind the soybeans with four or five cups water in a blender and

season them with salt. (Adding sesame seeds to the soybeans in the blender gives nice flavor.)

2 Cut the cucumber and egg sheet into thin strips. Divide the tomato into eight sections.

3 Cook the noodles in boiling water, rinse them in cold water and drain. Place the noodles in a wide dish, pour the soybean puree over them and top it with the cucumber, egg strips and tomato.

1 Boil the soaked soybeans for 15 minutes.

2 Grind the **#1** soybeans with water in a blender.

3 Strain the ground soybeans and season them with salt.

Noodles with Beans

Thin Noodles on a Wicker Tray

Rice Cakes
Sweets
Beverages

Half-Moon-Shaped Rice Cake
Songp'yŏn (송편)

Sweet Rice
Yakshik (약식)

Ingredients   5 cups rice, 1 tbsp. salt, food colors, 2 oz. mugwort, 10 chestnuts, ½ cup sesame seeds, 10 jujubes, 1 cup sweet bean flour, 1 tsp. salt, 2 tbsp. honey, 2 tbsp. sesame oil, ½ cup sugar

Method   **1** Wash the rice, soak it for a while and drain. Grind the soaked rice very finely adding salt and strain.
2 Peel the chestnuts, boil them and put through a sieve. Pit and chop the jujubes finely. Fry the sesame seeds and simmer the sweet bean flour with ½ cup sugar. Then mix each ingredient with salt and honey.
3 Divide the ground rice into three equal parts. Add the food color to one-third along with boiling water and knead it into dough. Add boiled chopped mugwort to the second part and knead. Add boiling water to the rest as it is and knead it into dough.
4 Fill the dough pieces with the **#2** filling and shape them into half-moon-shaped rice cakes.
5 Steam the half-moon rice cakes and brush them with the sesame oil.

1 Divide the rice flour into three equal parts. Knead each part into soft dough.

2 Fill the dough pieces with the chestnut, and jujube stuffings and make the half-moon-shaped rice cakes.

Sweet Rice

Ingredients   5 cups glutinous rice, 2 cups (dark brown) sugar, 3 tbsp. sesame oil, 3 tbsp. soy sauce, 10 chestnuts, 20 jujubes, 2 tbsp. raisin, ¼ cup pine nuts.

Method   **1** Soak the glutinous rice thoroughly in water and drain. Steam it with the chestnuts in a steamer. When steaming hot, sprinkle with salt and then dash cold water over the steamed rice and steam once more.
2 Pit the jujubes and cut them into 4 pieces.
3 Remove the tops of the pine nuts.
4 Scoop steamed rice out of the steamer while still hot and mix it with the jujubes, raisins, pine nuts, dark brown sugar, soy sauce and sesame oil evenly. Steam the mixture in greased pans in an electric oven at 450°F for 20 mi-

Glutinous Rice Cake
Injölmi (인절미)

1 Pound the steamed glutinous rice in a mortar.

2 Dip the pounded rice cake into water to shape into pieces and cut.

Ingredients 5 cups glutinous rice, 1 tbsp. salt, ½ cup dried sweet beans, ½ cup dried yellow bean flour, ½ cup dried green bean flour

Method **1** Soak the glutinous rice in water thoroughly and drain. Place it on a damp cloth in a steamer, leaving the center empty, and steam well. Sprinkle with salt water while steaming and stir with a wooden scoop.

2 Place the steamed glutinous rice in a mortar while still hot and pound until smooth.

3 Soak the sweet beans in water and remove the skins completely. Steam the beans and mash when hot. Push the mashed sweet beans through a thick sieve making a sweet bean puree. Wash the dried beans and drain, fry and grind them finely into the bean flour.

4 Remove the pounded rice cake from the mortar by dipping your hands in water; place it on a flat board. Shape it into thin, flat rectangles. Cut the rectangles into 1⅔″ long pieces and dip the rice cake pieces into the bean flour.

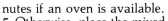

nutes if an oven is available.

5 Otherwise, place the mixed rice in a bowl and put the bowl into a steamer containing boiling water and steam. Fluff up the mixed rice several times while steaming.

6 When the rice gets tender, add the pine nuts, jujubes and raisins and pack the rice into greased jello-molds or custard cups. Then turn the packed molds upside down to remove the sweet rice and serve.

1 Soak the glutinous rice in water and steam it with the chestnuts in a steamer.

3 Stir the mixed rice up and down when steaming-hot sprinkling with salted water.

2 Pit the jujubes and remove the tops of the pine nuts.

4 When the rice is done, add all the ingredients and mix well.

5-Color Rice Cake Balls
Osaekkyŏngdan (오색경단)

3-Color Sweet Dumplings
Samsaekchuak (삼색주악)

Ingredients 5 cups glutinous rice, 2 cups dried sweet beans, 1 cup sugar, 1 tsp. salt, 10 chestnuts, 20 jujubes, ½ cup black sesame seeds, ½ cup soy bean flour, ½ cup cinnamon powder

Method **1** Wash the glutinous rice and soak it in water. Crush it finely adding salt and sift.
2 After cleaning soak the sweet beans in water and let them stand overnight. Boil, mash and sieve them. Squeeze the liquid from the sweet bean puree and simmer it with sugar to make the filling.
3 Peel the chestnuts, cut them into fine strips and soak them in cold water. Pit the jujubes and cut them into thin strips.
4 Remove the skins by rubbing the black sesame seeds together in water. Stir-fry and crush them.
5 Wash and dry the beans. Fry until golden brown, crush finely and sift them.
6 Knead the glutinous rice flour mixed with boiling water and fill small pieces of the dough with the simmered sweet beans to make small balls. Boil the balls in boiling water, rinse them in cold water, drain and let them cool. Then roll each ball in the chestnut strips, jujube strips, cinnamon, black sesame seeds or soy flour.

1 Knead the glutinous rice flour into dough.

2 Simmer the sweet bean puree with sugar.

3 Fill the dough with the sweet bean mixture to make the balls.

4 Boil the balls in boiling water and rinse them in cold water.

5 Roll the #4 balls in soy flour.

Ingredients 5 cups glutinous rice, 1 tbsp. salt, 20 jujubes, 1 tsp. cinnamon, 1 tsp. honey, food coloring (pink, green), 3 cups frying oil, ½ cup honey or syrup

Method **1** Wash the glutinous rice and soak it in water. Drain, grind finely and sift. Divide the sifted rice into three equal parts.
2 Dissolve each food coloring separately in water.
3 Leave one-third of the rice flour white, add the food coloring separately to the other two parts of

the rice flour. Add boiling water and knead each of them into dough.

4 Pit the jujubes. Chop finely and mix them with the honey and cinnamon to make the filling.

5 Shape the dough into dumpling filling them with the jujube mixture.

6 Heat the frying oil to 340°F and deep-fry the dumplings.

7 When the dumplings are done, take them out of the oil, soak them in honey-water and serve.

Hint Fry the dumplings a few at a time so that they do not stick together.

3-Color Sweet Dumplings

1 Chop the jujubes finely and mix them with the honey and cinnamon.

2 Knead the glutinous rice flour and fill the dumplings with the **#1** mixture.

3 Deep-fry the dumplings in oil at 340°F.

Ingredients   3 cups glutinous rice, 2 cups regular rice, 1 tbsp. salt, 1 cup jujube, 6 tbsp. sugar, 4 tbsp. honey, 5 chestnuts, 1 oz. mugwort, 1 tsp. cinnamon, 1 cup dried sweet beans, ½ cup pine nuts

Method   **1** Soak the glutinous rice and regular rice a long time in water. Grind very finely and sift. Divide the rice flour into two equal parts.

2 Mix half of the rice flour with the chopped mugwort; add enough hot water to knead it into dough. Mix the rest of the rice flour with the chopped jujubes; add enough hot water to knead it into dough.

3 Steam the **#2** dough in a steamer. Cut the steamed dough into bite-sized pieces. Mash the boiled chestnuts and cut the jujubes into fine strips. Then mix them with 3 tbsp. sugar and 2 tbsp. honey.

4 Soak the sweet beans in water and steam until very soft. Mash while still hot and sieve them to make a sweet bean paste.

5 Roll the pieces of **#3** jujube rice cake in the **#4** mixture. Roll the pieces of **#3** mugwort rice cake in the sweet bean paste and chopped pine nuts.

169

Chestnut Balls · Jujube Balls
Yullan·Choran (율란 · 조란)

Honey Cookies
Yakkwa (약과)

Ingredients   **A.** 30 chestnuts, 7 tbsp. honey, 2 tbsp. cinnamon **B.** 5 tbsp. chopped pine nuts, 20 jujubes, 1 tbsp. pine nuts, 3 tbsp. cinnamon

Method   **1** Peel and steam the chestnuts until tender and sieve while still hot. Mix the sieved chestnut with the **A** honey and cinnamon. Remove the tops from the pine nuts and chop them finely on paper.

2 Shape half of the mixture into chestnut-like balls and roll them in cinnamon or chopped pine nuts.

3 Shape the rest of the mixture into jujube-like balls. Roll half of the balls in chopped pine nuts and the rest in finely cut jujube strips. Slip a pine nut into one end of each ball.

1 Steam the peeled chestnuts and sieve.

2 Mix the #1 sieved chestnut with the honey and cinnamon.

3 Shape the #2 mixture into balls and roll them in jujube strips, cinnamon or chopped pine nuts.

Ingredients   1 cup flour, 1 tbsp. sesame oil, 1 tsp. salt, 2 tbsp. honey or syrup, 2 tbsp. rice wine, 2 tsp. cinnamon, 1 tsp. ginger juice, 1 cup grain syrup (like dark corn syrup), 1 tbsp. pine nuts

Method   **1** Combine the flour, sesame oil, honey, rice wine, 1 tsp. cinnamon and 1 tsp. ginger juice and knead well until the dough is smooth.

2 Press the dough into cookies by using an oiled yakkwa mold. Deep-fry the cookies in oil at 270-300°F, take them out of the oil, drain and soak them in grain syrup. Sprinkle the cookies with the finely chopped pine nuts.

Honey Cookies

Thin Cookie Twists
Maejagwa (매자과)

Ingredients   1 cup flour, 1½ tbsp. sugar, salt, 3 tbsp. rice wine, 2 tbsp. water, frying oil, dark corn syrup: (1 lb. black "yot"—a Korean candy base used in sweet syrups and candies—1 cup water, 1 cup sugar), chopped pine nuts

Method   **1** Mix the flour with the salt and sugar and sift.

2 Mix the sifted ingredients with the rice wine and ginger juice and knead the mixture into dough.

3 When the dough is smooth, roll it out into thin sheets and cut them into pieces ¾"×2". Slit each piece down the center leaving the ends intact and pull one end of each piece through the slit to make thin cookie twists.

4 To make the syrup boil the black "yot", water and sugar until thick on low heat.

5 Deep-fry thin cookies in oil at 300-320°F and soak them in the syrup.

Hint   Honey or sugar syrup can be used instead of grain syrup.

1 Add the sugar and salt to the flour and sift.

2 Cut the dough and shape it into thin cookie twists.

3 Deep-fry the cookies in oil at 300-320°F and soak them in grain syrup.

1 Knead the flour and seasonings into dough.

2 Press the dough into the yakkwa mold to form the cookies.

3 Deep-fry the cookies and soak them in grain syrup.

Candied Vegetables in Syrup
Kaksaekchŏnggwa (각색정과)

Patterned Savory Cakes
Osaektashik (오색다식)

1 Scald the carrot and radish and rinse them in cold water.

2 Simmer #1 and ginseng rootlets with sugar water and cook slowly adding the light syrup.

Ingredients   ½ cup black sesame seeds, 1 cup cornstarch, ½ cup dried green beans, ½ cup dried yellow beans, 1 tbsp. omija (a kind of seed-tea) juice, 1 cup corn syrup

Method   1 Wash the green and yellow beans and the black sesame seeds. Fry each separately, crush finely and sift. Knead the bean flour with the grain syrup and press the dough into patterned cakes by using the patterned-cake mold. Mix the sesame flour with some syrup, knead and press the dough into patterned cakes.

2 Mix ½ cup of the starch with some grain syrup, knead and form the dough into patterned cakes.

3 Mix the other ½ cup starch with some of the grain syrup and omija juice, knead well and form the dough into patterned cakes.

Patterned Savory Cakes

Ingredients ⅓ lb. rootlets of ginseng, 1 carrot, ½ Korean white radish, 2 tbsp. salt, 1 cup sugar, 1 cup water, 1 cup light syrup

Method **1** Wash the ginseng rootlets well.

2 Cut the carrot and radish into pieces ¼" thick by ⅓"×2⅓". Scald in boiling salted water and rinse them in cold water.

3 Simmer the ginseng rootlets and the **#2** ingredients in the sugar water on low heat in a thick pan. Then add the light syrup and cook slowly until no syrup remains and the rootlets are sticky.

Ingredients ½ cup white sesame seeds, ½ cup black sesame seeds, ½ cup light-brown syrup, ⅓ cup sugar

Method **1** Clean the white and black sesame seeds separately. Stir-fry them until plump.

2 Mix the syrup and sugar in a bowl and cook until clear. Mix the white sesame and black sesame each separately with the boiled syrup and roll out the mixture into thin sheets.

3 Place the black sesame sheet on the white sesame sheet and roll them together before they cool.

4 Roll in mat and slice into small circles.

1 Mix the white sesame and black sesame each separately with the boiled syrup.

3 Place the black sesame sheet on the white sesame sheet and roll them together tightly in the bamboo mat.

2 Roll out each mixture into a thin sheet.

4 Cut the roll into bite-sized circles.

1 Mix all the ingredients with grain syrup and knead into a soft dough.

2 Shape the dough into small patterned cakes using the patterned-cake mold.

Nine-Section Dish
Kujŏlp'an (구절판)

Ingredients   A. 3 oz. beef, 2 tsp. soy sauce, 1 tsp. chopped green onion, ½ tsp. chopped garlic, 1 tsp. sesame oil, ½ tsp. sesame salt, 1 tsp. sugar
B. ⅓ lb. shrimp, salt, sugar, vinegar
C. ½ cucumber, 3 oz. carrot, 2 tsp. salt, 2 tsp. sesame oil
D. 3 oz. bamboo shoots, 1 tsp. salt, 1 tsp. sesame oil
E. 6 dried brown, oak mushrooms, 1 tsp. soy sauce, ½ tsp. sugar, sesame oil
F. 1 egg, salt
G. 3 oz. bellflower roots, 1 tsp. salt, ½ tsp. sesame oil, ½ tsp. garlic
H. 1 cup flour, 1 cup water, salt
I. 1 tbsp. chopped pine nuts

Method   1 Remove the entrails from the shrimp. Insert toothpicks into the bodies of the shrimp and scald them in boiling water; remove the shells. Cut the flesh into thin strips and mix with the salt, sugar and vinegar.
2 Cut the beef into thin strips, season it with the **A** ingredients and fry.
3 Soak the dried mushrooms in water and cut them into thin strips. Season them with the **E** ingredients and fry.
4 Cut the carrot and cucumber into thin strips and sprinkle them with salt. Squeeze out the water and fry. Cut the bamboo shoots

into thin strips and fry.
5 Fry the beaten egg into a thin sheet and cut it into 2" long strips.
6 Scald and shred the bellflower roots finely. Fry in the sesame oil and mix them with the **G** ingredients.
7 Mix and beat the **H** ingredients until the batter is smooth. Drop the batter by spoonfuls onto a hot lightly oiled fry pan to make the thin pancakes.
8 Layer the pancakes in the center section of the 9-section dish topping each one with a little powdered pine nut. Then arrange the eight other prepared ingredients in the other sections.

1 Remove the shells from the boiled shrimps and season.

2 Cut the beef into thin strips, season and fry them.

174

Sweet Rice Drink
Shik'ye (식혜)

Ingredients   3 cups glutinous rice, 3 cups malt powder, 3 tbsp. pine nuts, 3 cups sugar, 40 cups water

Method   **1** Pour 40 cups of water over the powdered malt and let it stand for one night. Stir and press the malt-powder so that the malt-flavor seeps into the liquid. Strain the malt-water through a fine sieve and allow the malt-water to settle leaving a clear liquid.

2 Soak the glutinous rice in water and drain. Steam it in a steamer sprinkling some more water over the top when steaming-hot to produce more steam and sticky rice.

3 Place the steamed rice in a large bowl to cool. Add the clear malt-water to the bowl and stir it well. Then leave it at 100°F, until it ferments. (Or let it stand for two and a half hours or three hours in thermal rice container.)

4 When four or five grains of rice float to the top, take the liquid out of the container. As it cools, all grains of rice will float to the top. At this time, separate the grains from the liquid.

5 Wash the grains of rice in water and drain.

6 Simmer the fermented rice liquid and add the sugar to taste. Let it cool and store it in glass bottles.

7 Place the sweet rice drink in individual serving bowls and top it with some grains of the fermented rice.

Hint   Add a little ginger juice and float some minced citron with the grains of rice on the liquid for an even more delicious drink.

2 Add the clear malt-water to the steamed glutinous rice and stir well.

1 Press the malt hard in the water and strain the malt-water through a fine sieve.

3 When grains of rice float to the top, separate the rice and the liquid. Wash the grains of rice and simmer the liquid.

3 Cut the remaining ingredients into thin strips.

4 Mix the pancake batter.

5 Fry the batter.

Persimmon Punch
Sujŏnggwa (수정과)

Honey-Coated Pear
Paesuk (배숙)

Ingredients   10 dried persimmons, ⅓ lb. ginger, ¼ oz. stick cinnamon, 13 cups water, 2 cups sugar, 2 tbsp. pine nuts

Method   **1** Remove the seeds from the dried persimmons and replace them with four or five pine nuts.
2 Wash and scrape the ginger and slice it thinly. Simmer the ginger and stick cinnamon with the water until the strong taste draws well. Add the sugar and briefly boil again.
3 Pour this liquid through a fine sieve.
4 Pour this syrup over the dried persimmons in a large bowl.
5 When the persimmons are soft, serve them adding the syrupy liquid and sprinkling whole pine nuts on the top of each serving.

1 Remove the seeds from the dried persimmons and replace them with the pine nuts.

2 Simmer the ginger and cinnamon until the strong taste draws well.

Honey-Coated Pear

3 Cover the persimmons with the spicy syrup and store the remaining syrup separately.

Ingredients   2 firm Korean pears, ¼ oz. stick cinnamon, ¼ lb. ginger, 10 cups water, 1½ cup sugar, 3 tbsp. black pepper seeds, pine nuts
Method   **1** Scrape the ginger and slice thinly. Boil the ginger and cinnamon with the water.

Rice-Cake Fruit Cup
Ttŏk'wach'ae (떡화채)

1 Boil the sliced ginger and stick cinnamon with the water.

2 Divide the pear into eight equal sections, remove the center core and press in the black pepper seeds.

3 Place the pear pieces in a pot, sprinkle with sugar and allow them to stand for a while.

4 Pour the **#1** syrup over the pears and simmer on low heat.

2 Peel the pear and divide it into eight equal sections. Remove the center core and press three or five black pepper seeds into the pear pieces. Sprinkle with sugar and allow them to stand for a while. Add the **#1** syrup and simmer until the pear looks glazed. To serve, sprinkle whole pine nuts on top.

Ingredients   ½ cup glutinous rice flour, ½ cup rice flour, ½ tsp. salt, 2½ cup water, ½ cup sugar, 1 knob ginger, raisins, pine nuts, 1 apple, 1 plum, 1peach

Method   **1** Knead the rice flour, salt and hot water into a soft dough. Shape the dough into ginko nut-sized pieces. Place some raisins and pine nuts on each piece

1 Knead the rice flour, salt and hot water into a dough.

and re-shape into round balls.

2 Boil the balls in boiling water and rinse them in cold water.

3 Boil the water with the sugar and ginger to make a syrup and let it cool. Then remove the ginger from the syrup. Slice the fruits into bite-sized pieces. Place the rice cake balls, fruit pieces in a bowl and pour on the syrup to serve.

2 Slice the fruits into bite-sized pieces.

3 Boil the water with the sugar and ginger and let it cool.

Watermelon Punch
Subak'wach'ae (수박화채)

Ingredients 1 watermelon, 1 bottle cider, ½ cup brandy, 1 tbsp. pine nuts, 1 cup sugar, 1 cup water

Method **1** Cut the upper part of the watermelon in a sawtooth-design. Scoop out watermelon balls with a melon baller.
2 Boil 1 cup water with 1 cup sugar to make the syrup.
3 Soak the watermelon balls in the syrup. Wrap the remaining watermelon in a cloth and squeeze out the juice.
4 Place the watermelon balls, syrup, cider, brandy and **#3** watermelon juice in the watermelon shell and float ice pieces on top.
5 Serve the watermelon punch sprinkled with pine nuts in a bowl.

1 Cut the watermelon in a sawtooth-design.

3 Wrap the remaining watermelon in a cloth and squeeze out the juice.

2 Soak the watermelon balls in the syrup.

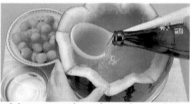

4 Mix **#2**, **#3**, brandy, cider and the syrup.

1 Layer the grapes and sugar in a large jar.

178

Grape Wine
P'odoju (포도주)

Plum Wine
Chaduju (자두주)

Ingredients   1⅓ lb. grape, ¼ lb. sugar, 1½ liter Korean soju (a strong rice-wine)

Method   **1** Wash the grapes. Pat dry with a cloth. Layer the grapes and sugar in a large glass jar and let them stand for a day.

Add a little Korean wine to dissolve the sugar and seal.

2 Two months later, take the grapes out of the jar and let them drip through a fine sieve. Place the strained grape wine in the bottle and seal.

1 Layer the plums and sugar, let them stand overnight and add Korean soju.

Plum Wine

2 Two months later, let the grape liquid drip through a fine sieve.

Ingredients   1⅓ lb. plum, ¼ lb. sugar, 1½ liter Korean soju (a strong rice-wine)

Method   **1** Wash the plums and pat dry with a cloth. Layer the plums and sugar in a large jar.

2 Allow the plums to stand overnight and then add Korean wine to the **#1** mixture.

3 When the plums ferment completely (one month later), place the plums over a fine sieve and let them drip. Place the strained plum wine in a bottle and seal.

179

Apple Wine
Sagwaju (사과주)

Ingredients 4 apples, ¼ lb. sugar, 1½ liter Korean soju

Method **1** Wash the apples well and dry them. Cut each apple into eight equal sections.

2 Layer the apples and sugar in a large jar and let them stand for two days. Then add 3 times as much Korean wine as the marinated apple pieces.

3 When the apples ferment (three months later), place the apple pieces over a fine sieve letting all the juice drip out. Place the strained apple wine in the bottle and seal.

Hint It is good to use a high proof alcohol, but Korean soju (a strong rice wine) is generally used.

3 Add 3 times as much Korean wine as the #2 mixture.

1 Wash the apples and dry them. Divide each apple into eight sections.

2 Layer the apples and sugar in a large jar.

4 Place the fermented apples over a fine sieve (three months later) and let the juice drip out.

Kimchi
Basic Side Dishes
Basic Sauces

Whole Cabbage Kimchi
T'ongbaech'ugimch'i (통배추김치)

Ingredients   2 heads Chinese cabbages, 2 cups coarse salt, 1 Korean white radish, 1 cup red pepper powder, ⅓ cup tiny salted shrimp, 2 knobs ginger, 1 head garlic, 1 large green onion, ¼ bundle very thin green onion, ⅓ lb. fresh oyster, ⅓ bundle watercress, 4 tbsp. salt, ¼ bundle Indian mustard leaf, red pepper threads

Method   **1** Trim the roots from the cabbages. Cut each cabbage lengthwise into two sections.
2 Make a brine with 10 cups water and 1 cup salt and soak the cabbage sections in the brine. Drain, sprinkle with the salt and let stand.
3 When the cabbages are well-salted and a bit limp, rinse thoroughly in cold water and drain.
4 Cut one-third of the radish into thin strips. Cut both kinds of green onions, the watercress stems and Indian mustard leaf into ¾" lengths.
5 Remove the shells from the fresh oysters and clean with salt water. Chop the salted shrimp, garlic and ginger.
6 Mix the red pepper powder well with the salted shrimp juice. Add the mixture to the radish strips and mix well until the reddish color is set. Then add the chopped shrimp, garlic, green onion, ginger, oysters, small green onion, Indian mustard leaf and watercress and mix well. Season with salt.
7 Pack the **#6** seasoned mixture between each leaf of the wilted cabbage. Cut the remaining radish into large pieces and mix it with the seasoned mixture.
8 Place the stuffed cabbages and radish pieces in a large crock and cover the top with cabbage leaves. Weigh it down with a clean, heavy stone.

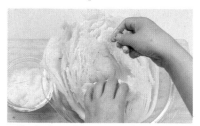

1 Soak the cabbages in salt water and drain. Sprinkle with salt and let stand.

2 Cut the radish, green onions and watercress and season.

3 Pack the seasoned mixture between each leaf of the cabbage.

Wrapped-Up Kimchi
Possamgimch'i (보쌈김치)

1 Soak the cabbage in salt water.

2 Cut all the ingredients and season.

3 Pack the #2 stuffing between each leaf.

Ingredients 1 head Chinese cabbage, 1 piece Korean white radish, 1 piece carrot, ½ bundle watercress, ½ octopus, 3 chestnuts, 2 dried brown, oak mushrooms, 2 stone mushrooms, ¼ pear, 1 cup coarse salt, 1 green onion, 2 cloves garlic, 1 knob ginger, 1 tbsp. pine nuts, red pepper threads, ½ cup red pepper powder, 2 tbsp. salted soused shrimp, 2 tbsp. salted anchovies, 1 tbsp. sugar, 2 oz. oyster

Method 1 Remove the outer leaves from the cabbage and halve it lengthwise. Soak it in salt water and let it stand for 6 hours.
2 Cut the radish, carrot and pear

into 1″ × 1¼″ square by ¼″ thick slices.
3 Soak the stone mushrooms and dried mushrooms in water and clean. Cut them into thin strips.
4 Remove the roots and the leaves from the watercress and cut the stems into 1¼″ pieces. Slice the chestnuts into flat pieces.
5 Clean the octopus rubbing it with salt and cut it into 1¼″ lengths. Cut the green onion, garlic and ginger into thin strips.
6 Wash the salted cabbage and drain. Cut the stem area into 2⅓″ pieces. Place the stem pieces on the outer leaves and wrap them

temporarily in the leaves.
7 Mix #2, #3, #4, #5 and oysters with the red pepper powder so that the ingredients pick up the reddish color. Season with the salted shrimp juice and salt, add the red pepper threads and pine nuts and mix well.
8 Pack the #7 stuffing between each #6 stem piece and this time wrap them firmly in the outer cabbage leaves.
9 Put the wrapped cabbage bundles one by one in a crock, pour the salt water over them and weigh them down with a heavy stone.

183

White Cabbage Kimchi
Paekkimch'i (백김치)

1 Sprinkle the cabbage with salt and let it stand.

2 Mix the sliced ingredients with the seasoning.

3 Pack the seasoned stuffing between the leaves of cabbage.

Ingredients   2 heads Chinese cabbages, 1 bundle watercress, 1 Korean white radish, 4 small green onions, 5 stone mushrooms, 1 pear, 5 jujubes, 3 chestnuts, ½ cup oysters, ⅓ octopus, 2 tbsp. salt, 1 head garlic, 3 knobs ginger, red pepper thread, 5 tbsp. salted soused shrimp, 2 tbsp. salted anchovies, 1 tbsp. pine nuts, MSG, 2 cups coarse salt,

Method   **1** Halve the cabbages lengthwise. Soak them in salt water for 6 hours and rinse them in cold water. Drain.
2 Cut the watercress and small green onion into 1⅔" lengths. Cut the trimmed stone mushrooms, chestnuts and jujubes into thin strips.
3 Cut the pear, garlic, ginger and half of radish into thin strips. Cut the rest of the radish into large pieces and sprinkle it with salt.
4 Wash the octopus rubbing it with salt and cut it into ¼" thick pieces. Wash well and rinse.
5 Remove the shells from the oysters, wash well and dry them off. Combine 1 cup of water and salted soused shrimp to make the salt brine.

6 Cut the red pepper thread enough so that they do not get tangled.
7 Mix the vegetable strips, octopus, oysters, pine nuts and red pepper thread thoroughly with the salt and MSG.
8 Pack the seasoned stuffing between each leaf of cabbage and wrap the cabbage with the outer

leaves. Layer the cabbage bundles and radish pieces in a large crock and pour the **#5** salt brine over them.

Radish Kimchi

Radish Kimchi
Yolmugimch'i (열무김치)

Water-Kimchi with Fresh Ginseng
Susamnabakkimch'i (수삼나박김치)

Ingredients 3 bundles young Korean white radish leaves, 1 bundle small green onion , 2 heads garlic, 1 knob ginger, 2 Korean green peppers, 2 red peppers, ½ round onion, powdered glutinous rice, 1 cup coarse salt

Method **1** Trim the young radish leaves and cut them into 2¾″ lengths. Soak them in salt water, wash and drain.

2 Wash the green onion, garlic and ginger. Cut the green onion into 2″ lengths. Chop the garlic and ginger. Cut the round onion into thin strips.

3 Remove the stems and the seeds from the green peppers and red peppers and cut them diagonally.

4 Add the **#2** and **#3** ingredients to the salted radish leaves and mix well. Boil the glutinous rice with water into a thin paste-like gruel. Season the gruel with salt and let it cool.

5 Place the **#4** radish kimchi in a crock and pour the **#4** paste-gruel over it. To serve, put a mixture of kimchi and liquid into a dish.

Hint A flour gruel can be used instead of the glutinous rice gruel.

1 Trim the young radish leaves and cut them into 2¾″ lengths.

2 Add the green peppers, red peppers, ginger and garlic and mix well.

1 Peel and trim the fresh ginseng.

2 Slice the ginseng, radish, carrot and cucumber.

3 Mix the **#2** ingredients with the vinegar, sugar and water.

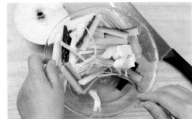

4 Add the sliced pear to the **#3** mixture.

Ingredients 4 roots fresh ginseng, ⅓ Korean white radish, 1 firm Korean pear, ½ carrot, 1 cucumber, 3 tbsp. coarse salt, 3 tbsp. sugar, ½ cup water, vinegar

Method **1** Peel the fresh ginseng. Remove the fine roots. Clean well and dry them off.

2 Cut the radish, carrot and cucumber into the same size as the ginseng pieces.

3 Add vinegar and sugar to the water and stir until the sugar dis-solves. Pour the liquid into a bowl and add the undried ginseng, radish, cucumber and carrot pieces.

4 Peel the pear, cut it the same size as the ginseng and add it to the **#3** mixture.

Hint When kimchi ripens into a sweet, vinegarish and salty dish, one can enjoy the true, refreshing kimchi flavor.

Whole Radish Kimchi
Alt'arigimch'i (알타리김치)

Radish Water-Kimchi
Tongch'imi (동치미)

Ingredients   2 bundles of small Korean white radishes, 2 oz. small green onion, 1 cup coarse salt, 1 cup red pepper powder, 3 green onions, 1 head garlic, 3 knobs ginger, 5 tbsp. salted soused anchovies, 1 tbsp. sugar

Method   **1** Trim the whole radishes and remove the outer leaves washing well. Sprinkle with salt and allow to stand.

2 Cut the green onions into thin strips. Chop the garlic and ginger finely.

3 Take two small green onions at

1 Trim and remove the outer leaves from the radish. Sprinkle them well with salt and let them stand.

Ingredients   10 Korean white radishes, 1 bundle small green onion, 1 firm Korean pear, 20 green thin Korean peppers, 5 red peppers, ¼ lb. ginger, 5 cloves garlic, 3 cups coarse salt, water

Method   **1** Select small, firm radishes. Remove the fine roots. Wash and drain.

2 Wash and tie the green onions together five at a time making bundles.

3 Slice the ginger and garlic thinly. Wrap the slices in gauze and tie.

4 Roll the radishes in salt. Place the radishes, **#3** ginger-garlic peeled pear and green peppers in

Radish Water-Kimchi

1 Roll the radishes in salt.

2 Tie the small green onions into bundles of 5 each.

3 Wrap the garlic and ginger slices in gauze and tie.

a time and make them into a small bundle.

4 When the radish is well-salted, wash it and drain to remove any excess water. Mix the salted radish with the red pepper powder until the color sets.

5 When the radish is deeply colored, add the chopped garlic, green onion, salt, salted anchovy juice, sugar and small green onion and mix thoroughly. Place the radish kimchi in a crock.

Hint Select radishes with fresh green tops and thick, stubby roots.

2 First mix the radish with red pepper powder and then add the remaining ingredients and mix thoroughly.

a crock and sprinkle with salt.

5 Three days later, pour salt water into the crock.

6 Cover the top with the radish leaves and weigh them down with something heavy.

Hint To store the vegetables in an underground pit, choose a dry place facing toward the south. Dig 2 meters deep, place the radish upside down, stack the carrots and put the cabbages in the middle. Cover and make a ventilating hole on the top.

4 Add enough salt water to cover the radishes.

Ingredients 3 cucumbers, 5 tbsp. salt, 2 green onions, 1 clove garlic, ¼ bundle small wild leeks, 1 round onion, 6 tbsp. red pepper powder, 1 tbsp. sugar, 1 tbsp. salted soused shrimp. 1 tsp. salt

Method **1** Clean the cucumbers rubbing them with salt and cut them into 2⅓" lengths. Cut long slits lengthwise through the cucumber, leaving the ends intact Sprinkle with salt and allow to stand for several hours.

1 Cut slits through the cucumbers, sprinkle them with salt and let them stand.

2 Chop the round onion , green onions and garlic. Cut the small leeks into ⅓" lengths.

2 Chop the green onion, garlic and round onion· finely. Cut the small leeks into ⅓" lengths.

3 Grind the red pepper powder with hot water in a mortar. Add the shrimp juice, small leeks, chopped round onion, garlic, green onion, sugar and salt to the ground red pepper powder and mix well.

4 Dry off the excess water from the salted cucumbers. Stuff the slits with the **#3** mixture.

3 Grind the red pepper powder and salted soused shrimps with hot water. Add the **#2** vegetables and mix well.

4 Dry the excess water from the salted cucumbers and stuff the slits with the **#3** mixture.

Hot Radish Kimchi
Kkakttugi (깍두기)

Dried Radish Strips in Soy Sauce
Muumallaengijangatchi (무우말랭이장아찌)

Ingredients   1 Korean white radish, ⅓ cup coarse salt, 2 cloves garlic, 1 knob ginger, 1 green onion, ½ cup red pepper powder, ¼ bundle watercress, 1 tbsp. sugar, 1 tsp. sesame seed, 1 tbsp. salted soused shrimp

Method   **1** Select plump, firm Korean radish. Cut the radish into cubes ¾″×1″. Sprinkle with salt and let stand.

2 Cut the green onion and water-

1 Cut the radish into cubes ¾″×1″.

Ingredients   ½ lb. dried Korean white radish strips, 2 cups soy sauce, 1 green onion, 1 clove garlic, 1 knob ginger, 2 tbsp. red pepper powder, 1 tsp. sesame salt, 3 tbsp. sugar, 1 tbsp. sesame oil, red pepper threads, MSG

Method   **1** Soak the dried radish strips in water and clean them rubbing them between your hands. Squeeze out the water.

2 Sprinkle the radish cubes well with salt and mix them with the red pepper powder.

3 Add the glutinous rice paste-gruel, sugar, salted shrimps, garlic and ginger and mix well.

Dried Radish Strips in Soy Sauce

1 Soak the dried radish strips in water and clean them.

cress stems into 2" lengths.

3 Mix the salted radish cubes with the red pepper powder. Boil the glutinous rice flour with water into a thin paste-gruel and let cool.

4 Add the green onion, watercress, garlic, ginger and glutinous rice paste-gruel to the colored radish and mix well. Season with salt.

Soak them in soy sauce and allow them to stand overnight.

2 Add the sugar, sesame oil, chopped garlic, ginger, MSG, red pepper threads and sesame salt and mix well.

2 Squeeze out the water and marinate them in soy sauce.

3 Mix the **#2** strips with the seasonings.

Cucumbers in Soy Sauce
Oijangatchi (오이장아찌)

Ingredients   10 dark green seedless cucumbers, 1 cup coarse salt, 3 cups soy sauce, 3 tbsp. sugar, 1 green onion, 2 cloves garlic, 2 tsp. sesame oil, red pepper threads, 1 tsp. sesame seed

Method   **1** Select fresh, long cucumbers. Sprinkle the cucumbers with salt, weigh them down with a heavy stone and let them stand for 10 days.

1 Sprinkle the cucumbers with salt, weigh them down with a heavy stone and let them stand for 10 days.

2 Cut the cucumbers into thin sticks and soak them in cold water to remove the saltiness.

2 When the cucumbers are well-salted, cut them into thin sticks and rinse to remove the saltiness.

3 Simmer 3 cups soy sauce and 3 tbsp. sugar in a pot and cool.

4 Pour the **#3** liquid over the salted cucumbers and let them stand overnight.

5 Remove the **#4** liquid and mix the cucumbers with the remaining seasoning.

3 Simmer the soy sauce and sugar and let it cool. Pour the liquid over the cucumbers.

4 Remove the **#3** liquid and mix the cucumber with the seasonings.

Sesame Leaves in Soy Sauce
Kkaennipchangatchi (깻잎장아찌)

Todok in Red Sauce
Tŏdŏkchangatchi (더덕장아찌)

Ingredients   200 sesame leaves, 1 tbsp. whole sesame seed, 1 head garlic, 1 cup soy sauce, 2 tbsp. sugar, red pepper threads, 1 red pepper, 2 tbsp. red pepper powder, 2 chestnuts, 1 knob ginger

Method   **1** Select tender sesame leaves. Wash them well and pat dry with a cloth.

2 Cut the chestnuts and garlic into thin strips.

3 Mix the soy sauce, red pepper strips, chopped ginger, sesame seed, garlic, chestnuts, red pepper threads, sugar and red pepper power to make the seasoning sauce

4 Place the sesame leaves one on top of the other in a bowl and sprinkle them with the seasoning sauce. Sprinkle all the sesame leaves with the seasoning sauce. Place them in a jar and weigh them down with a heavy stone.

1 Wash the sesame leaves and pat off excess water.

2 Make the seasoning sauce with all the ingredients.

3 Sprinkle the sesame leaves with the seasoning sauce.

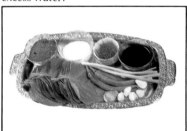

Ingredients   ½ lb. todok (a white root), 1 cup red pepper paste, 2 green onions, 3 cloves garlic, 1 tbsp. sesame salt, 1 tbsp. sugar, 1 tsp. sesame oil

Method   **1** Peel the todok and soak them in salt water to remove the bitterness. Pound the todok into flat, thin pieces with a round stick.

2 Dry excess water from the

Todok in Red Sauce

Sugared Seaweed
Miyŏkchaban (미역자반)

Ingredients   1 oz. brown seaweed, 2 tbsp. sugar, 4 tbsp. sesame oil, sesame seed

Method   **1** Cut the seaweed into bite-sized pieces.

2 Heat the sesame oil in a fry pan and add the seaweed pieces a few at a time and fry just until crisp.

3 Drain the fried seaweed pieces on paper to remove the oil. Sprinkle with the sugar and sesame seed.

Hint   This crispy seaweed (or fried tangle) may be crumbled onto hot boiled rice or stir-fried rice with vegetable.

1 Soak the todok in salt water to remove the bitterness.

1 Cut the seaweed into bite-sized pieces.

2 Heat the sesame oil in a fry pan and fry the seaweed pieces.

2 Dry excess water from the todok and pound it with a round stick.

3 Drain the fried seaweed pieces on paper and sprinkle with the sugar and sesame seed.

3 Mix the todok with the red pepper paste.

todok. Mix the dried todok with the red pepper paste and place it in a jar.

3 When the todok is deeply colored, take it out of the jar. Shred it finely and season it with the chopped green onion, sesame salt, sugar and sesame oil.

Hint   Add well-fermented red pepper paste to the todok.

Deep-Fried Laver
Kimbugak (김부각)

Deep-Fried Sesame Leaves
Kkaennippugak (깻잎부각)

Ingredients 20 sheets laver, ½ cup glutinous rice powder, 1 cup glutinous rice, ¼ cup sesame seed, 1 tbsp. sugar, 1 tbsp. salt, salad oil
Method 1 Boil the glutinous rice powder with salt and water to

Ingredients 20 sesame leaves, ½ cup glutinous rice powder, ½ cup glutinous rice, 2 tbsp. sesame seed, salad oil, 1 tsp. sugar, 2 tsp. salt
Method 1 Select tender and well-formed sesame leaves. Clean well and pat off excess water.

make a thin paste-gruel. Spread the paste on each sheet of laver, stick two sheets together and dry them in the sun.
2 Lay half of the dried laver sheets flat and spread the paste on one side of the sheets again. Then

1 Put the glutinuous rice paste on each sheet of laver and stick two sheets together.

2 Boil the glutinous rice powder with salt and water to make a thin paste-gruel. Steam the glutinous rice, adding salt water, in a steamer.
3 Brush the paste-gruel on half of the dried sesame leaves and sprinkle with sesame seeds. Put the steamed glutinous rice on the

sprinkle them with the sesame seed and dry in the sun. Spread the rest of the dried laver sheets with boiled glutinous rice and dry on a wicker tray. Cut the dried sheets of laver into bite-sized pieces and deep-fry in oil at 320°F.

2 Spread boiled glutinous rice on each sheet of laver, dry and deep-fry them.

rest of the sesame leaves. Place all the sesame leaves on a wicker tray and dry them in the sun.
4 Deep-fry them until crisp in oil at 360°F.
5 Sprinkle the deep-fried sesame leaves with salt and sugar while still hot.

Deep-Fried Laver

Deep-Fried Sesame Leaves

Salted and Spiced Oysters

Ŏriguljŏt (어리굴젓)

Salted Roe of Pollack

Myŏngnanjŏt (명란젓)

Ingredients   1 lb. oysters, 4 tbsp. salt, ⅔ cup red pepper powder, 1 tbsp. sugar, 1 clove garlic, 1 knob ginger

Method   **1** Wash the oysters in salt water and drain. Sprinkle the oysters with salt and let them stand for 2-3 days in a cool place.

2 Season the oysters with the red pepper powder, sugar, garlic and ginger. Place the seasoned oysters in a jar and store in cool place.

1 Wash the oysters in salt water and drain.

2 Season the oysters with the red pepper powder, sugar, garlic and ginger.

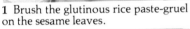

1 Brush the glutinous rice paste-gruel on the sesame leaves.

2 Sprinkle the sesame leaves with the sesame seed, dry and deep-fry.

Ingredients   ⅔ lb. roe of pollack, ½ cup red pepper powder, ½ cup salt, 2 heads garlic, 3 knobs ginger, sesame seed

Method   **1** Sprinkle the roe of pollack with salt and let it stand overnight.

2 Place layer upon layer of the roe in a jar adding the red pepper powder, chopped garlic, ginger and salt. Cover the top with vinyl and press it with a heavy weight. Three weeks later, sprinkle with the sesame oil and sesame seed and serve.

Salted Roe of Pollack

Pickled Crabs
Kejŏt (게젓)

Pickled Squids
Kkolttugijŏt (꼴뚜기젓)

1 Remove the shells from the crabs, clean them and cut them into pieces.

Ingredients 3 red crabs, 1 tbsp. sugar, 2 cups soy sauce, 3 cloves garlic, 1 knob ginger, 1 tsp. sesame oil, red pepper threads, 1 tsp. sesame seed, 2 tbsp. salt

Method **1** Wash fresh crabs and remove the shells. Cut them into pieces and sprinkle them with salt.
2 Mix the soy sauce with the garlic, red pepper threads, ses-

Ingredients ½ lb squid, 6 tbsp. red pepper powder, 2 tbsp. sugar, 1 tbsp. corn syrup, 5 cloves garlic, 1 knob ginger, MSG, 1 tsp. sesame oil, 1 tsp. sesame seed, ½ white Korean radish, 1 red pepper

Method **1** Remove the skin and the entrails from the salted squid. Cut them into thin strips and rinse them in cold water twice.

2 Mix the red pepper powder, chopped ginger, sugar, grain syrup, garlic, sesame salt and MSG to make the seasoning sauce.
3 Add the seasoning sauce to the squid and mix well. Then add sliced radish, red pepper and sesame oil and mix well.

1 Remove the skin and the entrails from the squid and cut into thin strips.

2 Add the seasoning sauce to the squid and mix well.

Pickled Squids

Salted Pollack Guts

Salted Pollack Guts
Ch'angnanjŏt (창란젓)

Salted Sole
Kajamishik'ae (가자미식해)

2 Pour the seasoning sauce over the crab pieces.

ame seed, ginger, MSG, sugar and sesame oil to make the seasoning sauce. Pour the seasoning sauce over the crab pieces, mix well and let them stand two hours before serving.

Hint One must eat the pickled crabs within a few days. For longer storage boil the soy sauce, cool it and pour it over the pickled crabs.

1 Cut the sole into pieces and sprinkle them with salt.

Ingredients 2 lb. guts (intestine) of walleye pollack, 1 cup red pepper powder, 2 heads garlic, 4 knobs ginger, 2 cups salt

Method **1** Clean the fresh fish guts. Wrap them in a cloth, weigh them down with a heavy stone and let stand overnight.

2 Sprinkle the well-dried guts with salt and allow them to stand overnight again.

3 Mix the salted guts with the chopped garlic, ginger and red pepper powder. Place the mixture in a jar and let stand for 15 days before serving.

Hint About 15 days later, take a little guts out of the jar, mix it with salted radish, garlic and red pepper powder and let it stand for 3-4 days before serving.

Ingredients 10 sole, 2 cups hulled millet, 2 cups salt, 2 heads garlic, 2 cups red pepper powder, 1 white Korean radish, 2 oz ginger

Method **1** Select small fresh sole. Scale the fish, remove the entrails, clean them and dry off excess water. Cut them into pieces and leave them under salt for 2 days. When the surface of the sole gets hard, drain them on a wicker basket. Boil the hulled millet leaving it a little bit hard; cool.

2 Mix the sole pieces with the

2 Mix the boiled hulled millet with the red pepper powder, ginger and chopped garlic.

3 Combine the **#1**, **#2** ingredients working in red pepper powder by hand.

boiled millet, garlic and red pepper powder. Place the mixture in a jar, cover the top with vinyl and weigh it down with something heavy.

3 When the sole ripens (two weeks later), cut the radish into thick strips, sprinkle it with salt and squeeze it tightly.

4 Mix the sole pieces with the radish strips, garlic, ginger and red pepper powder and check the seasoning. Place the mixture in a jar and seal.

4 Place the **#3** mixture in a jar and cover the top with vinyl. Weigh it down and let it stand for two weeks.

5 When the **#4** sole ripens, add the radish and mix well.

195

Fermented Soybean Lumps
Meju (메주)

Soy Sauce
Kanjang (간장)

Ingredients 18 lb. dried yellow soybeans

Method **1** Wash the soybeans and soak them in water overnight; drain.

2 Boil the soybeans in water on high heat. When they come to a boil, reduce the heat and simmer until the soybeans are thoroughly cooked. Drain the soybeans and pound them to a fine pulp while

1 Boil the soybeans thoroughly, drain well and pound them to a fine pulp while still hot.

Ingredients 2 fermented soybean lumps (9 lb.), 12 cups coarse salt, 30 liter water, 3 pieces of charcoal, 3 dried red peppers, 5 jujubes, 1 tbsp. sesame seed

Method **1** Remove the mold and the dust from the fermented soybean lumps two days before using. Wash them and dry them well in the sun.

2 Prepare a clean earthenware crock. Put the 12 cups of salt on a wicker basket and pour the water over it to make salt water. Let it stand overnight, so that any dregs settle to the bottom.

3 Put layer on layer of the soybean lumps in the crock and pour the strained salt water through a fine sieve into the crock.

4 Float the jujubes, dried red peppers and burned charcoal in the

Soy Sauce

1 Brush away the mold from the soybean lumps and wash.

2 Dry the soybean lumps in the sun.

3 Dissolve the salt in water and strain it through a fine sieve.

196

hot in a mortar.

3 Shape the soybean pulp into square lumps tamping it tightly; dry them in the sun.

4 Put them in a box placing straw between the lumps so they do not stick together. Seal the box and allow the lumps to ferment.

5 When the soybean lumps are covered with white mold, dry them well and store them in a bag.

2 Shape the pounded soybeans into square lumps tamping it tightly.

crock and sprinkle the salt on the top. Then seal the crock with gauze and allow it to stand covered for a few days.

5 After 3 days whenever the sun shines, open the lid to expose the contents to the sun; cover at night.

6 After about 40 days, carefully take the soybean lumps out of the crock and place them into another crock.

7 Strain the soy sauce through a fine sieve and pour it into a crock allowing the dregs to settle to the bottom.

8 Boil the soy sauce in a large pot skimming the froth from the top. Then simmer the soy sauce a long time.

9 Let the boiled soy sauce cool and pour it in the crock again. Expose it to the sun on shiny days.

Ingredients
2 fermented soybean lumps (9 lb.), 1 cup coarse salt, 3 cups powdered red pepper seed

Method
1 Mash the fermented soybean lumps which were left from making the soy sauce. Mix them with the powdered red pep-

1 Add the salt to the mashed fermented soybeans and mix well.

per seed and salt.

2 Pack the #1 mixture tightly in another crock. Sprinkle the top with quite a bit of salt.

Hint
Add some fermented soybean powder to the mashed soybean lumps and mix well for extra sweetness and nutrition.

2 Pack the #1 mixture tightly in a crock.

3 Sprinkle the top with quite a bit of salt.

4 Place the soybean lumps into the crock and pour #3 over them.

5 Add the jujubes, dried red peppers, charcoal and salt.

6 Skim the froth from the soy sauce and simmer.

Red Pepper Paste
Koch'ujang (고추장)

Ingredients   2 lb. fermented soybean powder, 6 lb. glutinous rice powder, 4 lb. red pepper powder, 5 cups malt, 6 cups coarse salt

Method   **1** Dissolve the malt in hot water and strain it through a fine sieve. Mix the malt water with the glutinous rice powder and stir well.

2 Boil the **#1** mixture on low heat to make a paste until golden brown and translucent; let it cool. If the paste is only half-boiled, it is apt to go bad.

3 Mix the paste first with the fermented soybean powder and stir well. Then add the red pepper powder and salt and stir well.

4 Cool the paste and add the fermented soybean powder.

Place the mixture in the crock and sprinkle quite a bit of salt on the top. Seal the top with gauze and expose it to the sun.

Hint   Break the half-fermented soybeans into small pieces and dry them in the sun. Pound them into powder and dry. This may be used to make the red pepper paste.

6 Season the **#5** mixture with salt and stir well.

1 Dissolve the malt in hot water and strain it through a fine sieve.

5 Add the red pepper powder to **#4** and stir well.

7 Place the red pepper paste in a crock and sprinkle salt on the top.

2 Add the glutinous rice powder to the malt water and stir well.

3 Boil the **#2** mixture on low heat until the paste becomes golden brown and translucent.

Table Settings

Dinner Table Setting
Pansang (반상)

  "Pansang" means a Korean table-set for a dinner. There are 3-chop, 5-chop, 7-chop and 12-chop settings according to the number of the side dishes. A 7-chop table includes seven side dishes along with boiled rice, soup, three seasoning sauces, and two heavy soups. On the table above, the hot radish kimchi can be replaced with vegetable salad, and one of the heavy soups with raw meat.

Menu: boiled rice, soup, soy sauce, vinegar-red pepper paste, kimchi, hot radish kimchi, hot pollack soup, rib stew, broiled beef patties, skewered beef and vegetables, boiled mussel, mung bean pancakes, seasoned cucumber with vinegar, and broiled fish.

Baby's First Birthday Table
Tolsang (돌상)

The "Tolsang" setting for celebrating baby's first birthday can be varied according to one's family circumstances and taste. This table includes not only food but also a writing brush, inkstone, book, cotton thread, money and archery bow, symbols used to wish the baby success, longevity and a happy future. This custom has been handed down from generation to generation.

Menu: noodles, stuffed jujubes, sweet glutinous rice cakes, steamed rice cake, half-moon-shaped rice cake, fruits, cookies, millet dumplings, glutinous rice cake coated with bean flour, and rice.

Bride's Gift Table
P'yebaeksang (폐백상)

   "P'yebaek" is a procedure wherein the bride makes a deep bow and offers her gifts to her parents-in-law. This custom is somewhat different according to the province and one's family. However, when the bride makes a deep bow to her parents-in-law, they throw jujubes in her skirt, wishing their descendants prosperity and good luck. The P'yebaek table is necessary for this formality.

How to wrap P'yebaek gifts in kerchieves: Make red and blue tasseled square kerchieves. Place the P'yebaek gifts on the tasseled kerchieves. Don't tie, but hold up, four edges of the kerchief together and fasten with a bond of white paper.
Menu: stuffed jujubes, broiled beef patties, chestnuts, nine section dish of delicacies, wine, chicken.

New Year's Day Table
Sŏlsang (설상)

The first day in January is New Year's Day. Since early times Koreans wear gala dress and perform memorial rites for ancestors and make a round of New Year's calls to elder members of the family and community. This table for guests is set and served with wholeheartedly buoyed up by hopes for the New Year.

Menu: rice cake dumplings, cookies, sesame cookies, sweet rice dish, sweet rice drink, skewered beef and vegetables, mung bean pancakes, steamed shrimp, fried rice cake, kimchi, hot radish kimchi, glutinous rice cake, boiled pork, nine section dish, red snapper casserole, broiled beef patties, wrapped-up kimchi, jujube balls, chestnut balls, water-kimchi, whole cabbage kimchi, coated sweet rice cakes, steamed shank of beef, soy sauce, vinegar-soy sauce, and rice wine.

Drinking Table
Chuansang （주안상）

The "Chuansang" table is set for appetizers served with drinks. The side-dishes can be varied according to the kinds of drinks. Prepare several special side dishes such as fried food, meat jerky, boiled pressed meats, hot stew and vegetable salad. Menu: dried side dishes, steamed lobster, mung bean pancake, skewered food, boiled pork, and wine.

GLOSSARY

Angelica Shoots (turŭp) are young shoots with tender green leaves of the angelica bush which are available fresh only in early spring.

Bamboo Shoots (chuksun) are the tender spring sprouts of the bamboo, off-white in color and shaped like a bud. Their flesh is tender but firm and should be scalded about 5 minutes in boiling water if used fresh.

Barley Tea (porich'a) is tea made from toasted barley kernels. It is prepared by adding the toasted barley to boiling water, boiling for 5 minutes, straining and serving. Barley tea is served cooled in the summer and warm in the winter. Corn tea is prepared and served the same way but is made from parched corn kernels.

Bean Curd (tubu) is a square or rectangular cake of pressed, coagulated soybean puree—the "cheese" of soymilk. It has a bland texture and is a very easy-to-digest, nutritious food. It should be kept in water (changing water daily) in the refrigerator.

Beans: There are a large variety of dried beans available in the Korean grain-bean shops. In addition there are various processed bean foods also available for daily use in the Korean diet.

   — yellow soybeans (hŭink'ong), sprouts (k'ongnamul), bean curd (tubu), soft bean curd (sundubu), bean paste (toenjang), fermented soybeans for making soy sauce (meju), seasoned fermented soybeans (ch'ŏnggukchang), soybean flour (k'ongkaru), soy sauce (kanjang).

   — Brown soybeans (pamk'ong—literally "chestnut beans") are a chestnut brown color and have a smooth chestnut-like texture when cooked.

   — Black soybeans (kŏmŭnk'ong) are served as a side dish.

   — mung beans (noktu), sprouts (sukchu namul), jellied mung bean puree (ch'ŏngp'o), mung bean flour (noktu karu).

   — red kidney beans (kangnamk'ong)

Bean Sprouts (k'ongnamul) may be grown at home, if desired, in a warm, wet jar or purchased in most vegetable sections of grocery stores. The large sprouts are from the yellow soybean; the smaller more delicate sprouts are from the green mung bean.

Bellflower Root (toraji) is a white root from the mountainside bellflower.

Bracken (kosari) is the early spring shoot of the fern plant. These shoots are gathered in the spring and sold fresh at that time. They are also dried for re-hydration later in the year. There is a common variety and a rather special royal fern variety that has larger, softer shoots.

Burdock Root (uŏng) is a long, fat nutritious root with a distinctive flavor which is washed, scrubbed and scraped, soaked in vinegar-water so that it does not change color and then cut into thick strips for use.

Chinese Cabbage (paech'u) is a solid, oblong head of wide stalk-leaves with a subtle flavor used widely in making kimchi.

Chinese Noodles (tangmyŏn) are very thin transparent noodles made from mung bean flour. They are sold dried in long loops. They should be soaked in warm water before use and cooked quickly. When cooked they become opaque and slippery.

Cinnamon (kyep'i) is a rough brown bark. It can be used whole or dried and ground to use in seasoning.

Eggplant (kaji) is the long, purple, shiny fruit of the eggplant plant; it is not large and round but sleek and elongated with a slight bulbousness at the end opposite the stem.

Garland Chrysanthemum (ssukkat) is a pungent, edible variety of Chrysanthemum; the leaves are used for seasoning and decorating like lettuce leaves in Korean recipes.

Garlic (manŭl), related to the onion, has a bulb made up of several cloves with a strong odor and flavor. It is widely used as seasoning in Korean dishes after being finely chopped. Garlic is also served pickled and its long green stems are eaten raw or boiled.

Ginger Root (saenggang) adds zip to many Korean dishes. Fresh ginger root has a thin light-brown skin over knobby bulbs. It may be washed and dried and placed in the freezer in a plastic bag. It is then available for grating into whatever dish is being prepared. It may be dried and powdered but fresh ginger is called for in most Korean recipes.

Gingko Nuts (ŭnhaeng) are oval-shaped, yellowish nuts with a soft texture. The shelled nuts may be stir-fried until green after which the outer skin will peel off easily. The peeled nuts are used for garnish on many special Korean dishes.

Ginseng (insam) is a much-prized root cultivated in Korea and China. This perennial herb is used mostly for medicinal purposes and is widely acclaimed for its rejuvenating qualities. It is usually sold dried, but fresh roots and rootlets are used in cooking. Ginseng tea and wine are popular in Korea.

Glutinous Rice (ch'apsal) is a white rice with a sticky consistency when cooked.

Glutinous Rice Flour (ch'apsal karu) is the flour from glutinous rice which is used in making Korean rice cakes.

Grain Syrup(choch'ong) is similar to dark corn syrup and is used as a sweetener. It is made by boiling "yot," a Korean candy base, with water and sugar until thick. Honey or sugar syrup can be used instead of this grain syrup in most recipes.

Green Onions: There are many varieties of green onions in Korea.
- (ch'ongp'a)—a medium sized variety harvested in the spring
- (puch'u)—a small, wild leek with a pungent flavor
- (shilp'a)—a thread-like onion with a taste similar to but stronger than chives
- (tallae)—a small, wild onion from the mountain meadows

Green Peppers, Korean (p'utkoch'u), are long, narrow unripe chili peppers and are usually hot to taste.

Indian Mustard Leaf (kat) is a green leaf available spring and autumn; Japanese "haruna."

Jujubes (taech'u) are similar to a date, usually used dried, for cooking or medicinal purposes. They should be soaked before using.

Kimchi is a spicy, slightly fermented pickle like vegetable dish accompanying every Korean meal. It is made from Chinese cabbage, Korean white radish, cucumber or other seasonal vegetables which are wilted with salt, stuffed with seasoning such as red pepper powder, chopped garlic, ginger juice and soused salted shrimp juice and fermented in earthenware crocks.

Konyak is jellied potato puree; it is sliced and used somewhat like a noodle.

Laver (kim) is cultivated carefully in the seabeds offshore in Korea and is of excellent quality. It is sold in packages of folded paper-thin sheets. It is used for wrapping rice rolls or broiled to a delicate crispness and served with a rice meal.

Lotus Root (yon-gun) is the root of the lotus flower. It is grey on the outside but when cut open a beautiful lacy effect is formed in each slice by several open tubes which run the length of the root. It is served as a vegetable or candied as a sweet.

Malt Powder (yotkirum) is dried sprouted barley which has been crushed into a powder. It is used to aid fermentation in making wines and drinks; it is a good food for yeast.

Mushrooms: There are several varieties used both fresh and dried.
- Brown oak mushrooms (p'yogo) (Japanese shiitake) are used in meat dishes after soaking well in warm water.
- Stone mushrooms (sogi) also should be soaked before using.
- Jew's ear mushrooms (mogi) are large, delicate ear-shaped fungi.
- Pine mushrooms (songi) grow on pine tree trunks; they are most often sold fresh or canned; very tasty when sliced and sauteed.

Pear, Korean (pae) is a crisp, large, round, firm, sweet, apple-like pear which is very juicy. It has a tan outside skin and a cream-colored flesh with dark brown seeds. Harvested in the fall it keeps well in rice-hulls in a cool place. It is considered to be an aid in digestion.

Pine Nut (chat) is the nut-like edible, soft-textured, somewhat oily seeds of the pinon tree. They are used to make a gruel-soup and in garnishing drinks and other foods.

Pine Nut Powder is ground or finely chopped pine nuts used for rolling sweet rice cakes and other delicacies.

Pulgogi is Korea's best-known charcoal-broiled marinated beef dish. It is traditionally broiled over charcoal in a slotted pan but it may be oven-broiled or quickly pan-broiled.

Radish, Korean White (muu) is a round, long, firm white root much larger than a red or white table radish. The taste is sweet when first harvested and its texture is crisp and juicy. It is a basic kimchi ingredient; it is sometimes dried for making soups in the winter and small, young radishes are used for a special spring kimchi.

Red Pepper Paste (koch'ujang) is a dark reddish paste made from fermented soybean and red pepper powder mixed with glutinous rice flour and malt. It is spicy hot and widely used to thicken and season soups and stews. It will keep well in the refrigerator.

Red Peppers (koch'u) are a basic Korean seasoning ingredient. They are small, long peppers similar to cayenne and are hot to the taste. They are dried and ground or cut into threads or used fresh for seasoning or garnish. They are very high in vitamin A.

Rice Cake (ttok) is a delicacy served at most celebrations in Korea. It is made by steaming a glutinous rice flour dough which has been filled or mixed with various foods such as sesame seed, beans, mugwort, nuts, jujube, raisins; the dough is usually shaped beautifully into half-moons, circles or other soft shapes.

Rice Wine (ch'ongju) is a clear white wine made from rice used for drinking and cooking.

Salted Soused Shrimp (saeujot) are tiny shrimp which have been salted and become somewhat pickled and juicy; used in making kimchi and in seasoning.

Sesame Leaves (kkaennip) are the beautifully shaped pungent leaves of the sesame plant which are served as a vegetable in a sauce or deep-batter-fried.

Sesame Oil (ch'amgirum) is pressed from toasted sesame seeds. It has a unique flavor and only a little is needed to add an authentic taste to Korean dishes.

Sesame Salt (kkaesogum) is a mixture of toasted, crushed sesame seeds and salt. Add 1 teaspoon of salt to each cup of seeds. It is a basic Korean seasoning.

Sesame Seeds: White (hŭinkkae), black (kŏmŭnk-kae) and round brown (tŭlkkae) are all used in Korean seasoning and in Korean candy-cookies.

Shinsollo is the name of a one-dish meal which is cooked at the table in a brass brazier "hot pot" which holds the charcoal in the center allowing the food to cook around it in a well-seasoned broth. It is a special occasion dish requiring hours of preserving preparation so that each food is cut precisely to the right shape and partially pre-cooked to allow for just the right last minute cooking at the table.

Soybean Paste (toenjang) is a thick brown paste made from a mixture of mashed fermented soybean lumps (left from making the soy sauce), powdered red pepper seeds and salt. It is used as a thickener for soups and stews and will keep well in the refrigerator.

Soy Sauce (kanjang) is a brownish-black salty liquid made by cooking fermented soybean cakes with water and salt. Each household in Korea used to make their own soy sauce in the spring; some

still do. These are mild and add good flavor to most any food. Soy sauce is used in cooking, especially meats, but is also placed on the table to use as a dip for sauteed vegetables, fish and meat. The Japanese soy sauce is less salty but sweeter than Korean soy sauce.

Sweet Red Beans (p'at) are small and round and used widely in Korean confections. When cooked and mashed they are sweet and soft-textured. This sweet bean puree is used as filling in rice cakes and also now in donuts and rolls.

Todok is a fibrous white root found in the mountain in the spring. It must be pounded with a mallet and washed with salty water to take away its puckery taste before seasoning and cooking. It is an appetite stimulant.

Watercress (minari) is an aromatic plant used frequently in Korean cooking, especially the stems. It is not exactly the same as watercress but almost. The delicate leaves may be added to soups and are good with fish.

Most, if not all, of these ingredients may be purchased in Oriental groceries.

INDEX

INDEX OF KOREAN RECIPE TITLES